ENERGY RESOURCES AND ECONOMIC DEVELOPMENT:
A Study of Rajasthan

Energy Resources and Economic Development

A Study of Rajasthan

N.R. KASWAN

CONCEPT PUBLISHING COMPANY, NEW DELHI 110059

The Indian Council of Social Science Research gave the financial support towards the publication of this work. However, the responsibility for the contents of the book — facts, opinions, conclusions, etc. — is entirely that of the author and not of the ICSSR.

ICSSR Consultant: **Prof. Moonis Raza**

ISBN 81-7022-387-3

First Published 1992

Published and Printed by
Ashok Kumar Mittal
Concept Publishing Company
A/15-16, Commercial Block, Mohan Garden
NEW DELHI-110059 (India)

Lasertypeset by
Microtech Advance Printing Systems (P) Ltd.
H-13, Bali Nagar
NEW DELHI-110015

PREFACE

THE GROWING awareness among researchers regarding the widening gap in levels of development between advanced and less-developed countries, and between regions within the less-developed countries, have taken into consideration various problems involved in the development process. The problem of Energy Resources has been taken into account with special emphasis on electricity supply, in the present study.

It is argued that the prosperity of the developed countries is somehow dependent upon the continued poverty of the less-developed nations, but it is essential in long-term interests of world society to encourage the development process keeping in view the fact that poverty anywhere is a threat to prosperity everywhere. Hence, economic-development is now termed as poverty eradication.

The terms growth, development and progress are often used inter-changeably, but these are not identical in meaning. Dudley Seers wrote 25 years ago about 'growth without development'. A simple indicator of the economic growth of a country will be the rate of change of GNP. Growth means the increase in a measurable variable. Development includes the growth, but is conceptually based on a wider range of variables. Development means economic transformations, whereas progress means social transformation. Progress is a wider term including within it the development factors as well as other social components. Progress is a continuous never-ending process. It is relative and not absolute. We cannot stop at a certain destination.

Economic development of Rajasthan refers to the problems of underdevelopment or less developed sectors of economy and the less developed regions of the State. The raising of economic levels is generally called economic growth in rich countries and in poor ones it is called economic development. Seven sectors of the economy of Rajasthan, have been taken into account for the evaluation of economic development of the State keeping in view the growth of energy utilization.

Energy is considered as an index of economic development. For an overall development of Rajasthan it is essential to ensure adequate and sustained supply of energy to urban and rural areas for every sector of economy. Both in its overall and per capita energy resources Rajasthan is among the most poorly endowed States in India. The State is rich in terms of mineral resources and poor in terms of conventional energy resources. The present work deals with electricity supply pattern in various sectors in Rajasthan making an attempt to find out the levels of economic development.

The work is divided into seven chapters. Chapter 1 is intended to introduce the nature of research, objectives of the study, data-base, method of investigation and the energy resources of Rajasthan. The power supply system (energy-network) has been discussed in Chapter 2. Chapter 3 presents the growth and demand pattern of power in Rajasthan. Energy consumption pattern has been analysed in Chapter 4. The urban power consumption pattern with two case studies of Ganganagar and Jaipur cities, have been dealt with in Chapter 5. Chapter 6 deals with the energy differentiation pattern in Rajasthan and Chapter 7 concluded the levels of electrification and the correlation between power and progress of Rajasthan.

I am highly indebted to my teacher and supervisor of this work, Dr. R.B. Singh for providing every possible guidance in the successful completion of this work. It would have not been possible for me to prepare this thesis without his encouragement and valuable guidance. I express my sincere gratitude to him. I also take this opportunity to express my thanks to statisticians of the RSEB for their constant help and cooperation in making available the relevant information and schedules. I also wish to thank the librarians of RSEB as well as Directorate of Economics and Statistics, for their valuable cooperation. My sincere thanks are due to my friends and family members who helped me in the preparation of this work. Though I am indebted to all of them for their cooperation, but the responsibility for any error in the present work is entirely mine.

Last but not the least, my sincere thanks are due to Shri Virendra Singh (Computer Services) for computerised printing of this manuscript with great interest and enthusiasm.

N.R. KASWAN

CONTENTS

LIST OF TABLES

LIST OF FIGURES

1

INTRODUCTION

THE PRESENT study is an attempt to measure the inter-sector and inter-district levels of energy consumption in Rajasthan and to compute its rate of growth and pattern of demand. Rajasthan is the second largest State in the Indian union with an area of 3,42,239 sq km taking up 10.4 per cent of the whole country. The area (23°30′-30° 12′ N. Lat. and 69°30′ -78° 17′ E.Long; Fig. 1.1)[1] is marked by extreme aridity and sandy deposits in the West, the Vindhyan scarpland and the Deccan lava plateau in the south-east and the eastern plains lie to the east of the oldest Aravallies extending diagonally across the State from Sirohi to Alwar district. The climate of Rajasthan is characterised by great extremes of temperature, long periods of severe drought accompanied by high winds, arid and semi-arid conditions of humidity. So, climatically Rajasthan is the driest State in the country. It has wide variations in the distribution of rainfall ranging from 16.4 cm in Jaisalmer to 100.47 cm in Jhalawar.[2] The districts covering 59 per cent of net area sown of the State are located in the western Thar, which hardly receives more than 33 cm of rainfall. The insufficient and erratic monsoon inevitably cast its gloom on the outlook of agriculture which is the back-bone of the State's economy. The contribution and effect of agriculture on the economy of the State is obvious from the figures of State Domestic Product, as it shared 45.38 per cent during 1985-86 (at current prices). Next to agriculture, industries and mining constitute the most important sector of State's economy. The State is endowed with rich mineral base, although it has yet to be fully explained. This sector contributed 21.47 per cent of NSIP in 1985-86 followed by 15 per cent from services group and 18 per cent from transport and communication.[3] Energy sector holds the key to the economy of the State which is reflected in its economic-activities. The focus of the present study is to assess the patterns of electricity utilization as an indicator of economic development, at sectoral and district level, for various points of time.

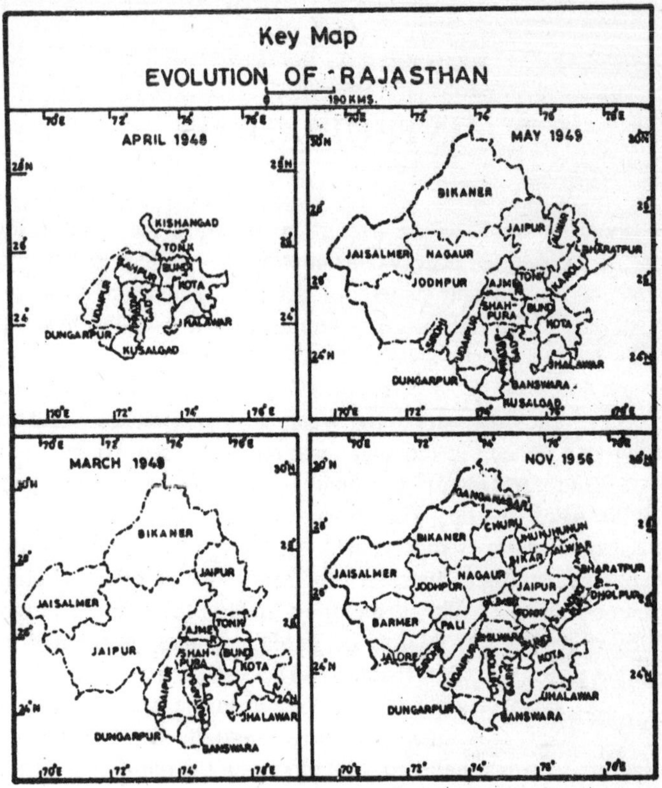
Key Map
EVOLUTION OF RAJASTHAN
APRIL 1948
MAY 1949
MARCH 1949
NOV. 1956

FIG 1.1

Nature of Research

A survey of research in energy studies shows a bulk of literature dealing with a variety of themes. The energy literature is highly fragmented, rarely developed and unifying conceptualisations. It needs to be identified the themes of research in a theoretical framework.

Energy has been studied as a topical field in engineering, economics, planning and to some extent in geography. Energy studies have long played a major role in the fields of engineering and technology, its emergence into social sciences is more recent. Within the social sciences, the interest in energy studies was primarily stirred in economics. Energy has been conceived as an area of research, where analytical and quantitative studies have an edge over descriptive and qualitative approach. Quantification, as a matter of fact, early started in economics, which provided a suitable nurturing ground within the social sciences for its germination and early growth. Major emphasis in connection with energy studies has been to develop models, equations to determine the location of economic activities, energy demand, energy elasticity and energy forecasting. With the emergence of quantitative revolution in geography, however, the energy studies lagged behind in comparison to other branches of economic geography.

A systematic approach to the study of energy with reference to spatial interaction was postulated by Chapman. The application of quantitative techniques to the analysis of energy network has been attempted in many recent studies. Several methods have been evolved to measure the efficiency of energy network in their entirety or its parts.

James O'Toole (1976) pleads the future economic growth that is not rooted in statistics gathered before the price of oil soared in late 1973. His study features technological forecasts, economic and social forecasts and suggests to choose right technologies. His particular contribution to the energy debate lies in its call for a redirection of attention to options that are realizable within the framework and the limits of the existing systems. Other studies of a similar nature include works done by Hitch (1978), Tanzer (1974) and Schumacher (1982).

Increasing energy consumption has been linked with economic progress. Tyner (1978) explores the relationship between energy resources and economic development in India. Studies of this type include those by Kirit S. Parikh, National Council of Applied Economic Research (1960, 1966), and topical studies such as Moulik

(1982) who compiled socio-economic aspects of biogas energy programme in India.

Slesser (1978) tries to explain in plan language what energy is, what it does and how it enters into the economic process. His work is attempted to analyse energy in relation to production and investment, space and time, substitution and conservation and what part it plays in the economic process.

The role of animate and inanimate forms of energy in increasing agricultural productivity in India has been examined by Shafi (1985). A similar study by Sheikh (1983) and Sharma (1986) attempted to analyse the role of farm power in agricultural development in Rajasthan.

Sathe (1987) stressed the importance of development of non-conventional energy resources. He pointed out that decentralised systems based on solar, wind, biomass, mini-hydle etc. hold a great promise and have shown encouraging results in rural areas, far-flung and isolated pockets where reaching electricity by the conventional method is proving extremely costly and time-consuming. The ultimate solution for achieving accelerated and all-round economic development lies in making these areas energy self-sufficient in as short a time as possible.

Objectives of the Study

Disparities in availability of power and consumption of power constitute an important factor in explaining variations in regional economic growth pattern in Rajasthan. It is necessary to know the levels of electricity flow while talking about economic development of a region. The focus of the present study is to assess sectoral and areal power consumption pattern keeping in view that some of the areas have developed at faster rates, while others have remained backward. Rajasthan is one such State in India where a lot of variations in economic development and power-consumption are found, partly because of variations in its physical endowments and partly due to varying spatial socio-economic infrastructures.

The changes in the level of economic development of a region can largely be understood through changes in the ways of power consumption. For the analysis of changes in power-consumption pattern, it is necessary to identify the areas of low and high power consumption, which would cast light on the rate of growth of a particular region compared to the other region.

Areal and sectoral imbalances in the supply and consumption of power is a common feature of the economic scene of Rajasthan. Gap between supply and demand of power is recurrent phenomenon. For any policy recommendation, it is necessary to assess the causes of high and low level of consumption of power. The present study is an attempt in this direction.

Power is the most important component of economy in developing a region. The variations in the levels of consumption of power over the years, indicate patterns of change in the sectors of economy of the area under study. The present study is an attempt to measure the district level pattern of power consumption, so as to analyse the regional disparities of economic development for various points of time. The power sector in any growing economy like ours is much more important because it provides the basic requisite quantum of energy not only for industrial, agricultural, commercial and domestic activities, but also for public lighting and drinking water supply systems. Electrical power is considered as an indicator of economic development of Rajasthan under these six sectors.

The purpose of this research has been to explore the relationship between energy resource development (taking into consideration the supply of electricity) and economic development (considering the six economic sectors) in Rajasthan. The work which evolved from the research is that energy resource development has lagged behind and constrained the economic development in Rajasthan. Inadequate attention has been paid to developing the power sector, both in terms of conventional and alternative non-conventional sources of power. This research consists of an analysis of power supply covering each of the major economic sectors in all the districts of Rajasthan.

The Choice of Area under Study

The rationale behind choosing Rajasthan as the area of study is as follows:

The State covers 10.43 per cent area of the country providing shelter for 5 per cent of her population. This is the second largest State-area after Madhya Pradesh extending through seven latitudes and nine longitudes covering an area of 3,42,239 sq km. The area of Rajasthan is 17 times greater than that of Israel, five times of Sri Lanka, three times of Chekoslovakia and more than the double that of

England. This vast area is trailing behind in the race of development.

The State is quite unique in its physical factor endowments, having 59 per cent land in dry region, the Thar Desert. Its Maru (deserts), Meru (mountains), Mal (plateaus) and Maidan (plains) vividly differentiate the economic growth and consumption patterns of power. The western part of the State is quite different from the eastern part from the view point of rainfall distribution, irrigation facilities, soil types, agriculture productivity, industrial development and population distribution.

Being the second most important State of India from mineral resources points of view, Rajasthan is endowed by nature with variety of mineral resources. Adequate supply of power is needed for the extraction and exploitation of these resources. So, the energy studies are of greater significance for the State of Rajasthan. The types and levels of power consumption not only differ from region to region within the State but also over points of time because of unequal distribution of energy resources and interdependent inter-State partnership in power distribution.

The most notable fact about the energy situation in Rajasthan is the dominant role of the non-commercial sources. It is important to note that the share of energy from non-commercial sources has been declining steadily. Electricity generated from hydel, thermal and atomic power plants is the principal secondary source of commercial energy in the State. The present study aims to examine the energy situation in terms of electricity supply pattern for the area selected for this purpose.

The Choice of Years

The nine points of time viz., 1959-60, 1964-65, 1969-70, 1974-75, 1979-80, 1984-85, 1989-90, 1994-95 and 1999-2000 which have been selected for the present study cover the periods of isostasy in demand and supply, period of widening gap and the period of forecasting. The selected years till 1975 were the normal years from the climatic point of view. During this span of time the demand and supply of power was more or less balanced. After that the increasing requirement of power in various sectors started to widen the gap between demand and supply. The period upto 1985 was selected to see the pattern of development of power of various sectors and short term prediction computed using extrapolation regression analysis.

While calculating areal differentiation at district level, the points of time have been selected on the basis of availability of data. District level data were found off the record prior to 1974 except the electrification of wells in rural sector. Maps are based on the availability of data.

Sources of Data

Data compiled and utilized for this study have been collected from various sources. All the relevant data regarding power generation, power availability and supply, power-consumption, number of consumers benefited, localities electrified, tube-wells energised, revenue assessed etc. have been extracted from Annual Statistical Reports published by Rajasthan State Electricity Board. Monthly informations of power supply is collected from unpublished records of the Board.

Data regarding population, livestock and number of villages have been collected from Census Reports of Rajasthan. Data pertaining budget distribution and fund allocation to power sector under five-year plans, are taken from "Progress Reports on Five Year Plans", published by Planning Department, Government of Rajasthan.

Other information about the area and topic under study, have been collected from Directorate of Economics and Statistics, Rajasthan, Jaipur and regional offices of RSEB at District Headquarters. Data have been compiled, categorised and tabulated sector-wise, and district-wise which are given in appendix.

Limitations of Data

While interpreting the results, the following limitations of the data may be kept in view. Firstly, the entire analysis is based on only one form of energy, that is the electricity. It is important to note that the study did not take into account all the forms of energy and hence the picture may be only a partial one. But its feasibility and accessibility would throw adequate light on the problem under consideration inspite of this limitation.

Method of Investigation

To explore the relationship between energy consumption and economic development, various themes have been evolved in energy studies. The present study is an out-come of a large scale analysis of spatial distribution pattern of sectoral power supply in Rajasthan. Power has been considered in terms of electricity supply to all the major economic sectors in the State. The study is designed into two major parts (1) sectoral analysis and (2) areal analysis of power consumption and growth pattern at district level. The following features have been taken into consideration while analysing the growth and consumption pattern of power in the area under study.

(i) Sectoral power consumption within the area and period under study.
(ii) Sectoral number of consumers within the area and period under study.
(iii) Sector-wise variations in the growth of power consumption.
(iv) Sector-wise per cent variation in the growth of power consumption.
(v) Sector-wise percentage variation in the growth of number of consumers benefited.
(vi) District-wise per capita power availability in Rajasthan.
(vii) District-wise distribution of power consumption.
(viii) District-wise sectoral distribution of power consumption.
(ix) District-wise distribution of consumers benefited.
(x) District-wise localities electrified.
(xi) District-wise wells energised 1968-1986.
(xii) District-wise distribution of transmission network.

These variables have been taken into account to analyse and evaluate the trends of power consumption of the following sectors:

(i) Domestic Sector
(ii) Commercial Sector
(iii) Industrial Sector
(iv) Agricultural Sector
(v) Public Lighting Sector
(vi) Water Supply Sector
(vii) Mix Load Consumers.

District-wise sectoral power distribution and transmission network system has been calculated in percentage of aggregate supply system of the region, on the basis of which maps have been prepared. To compute the sector-wise and aggregate growth-rate of power consumption and to calculate the future demand of power the Semi-logarithmic Exponential forms[4] have been taken into account.

$$y = a + b.t \tag{1.1}$$
$$Gr = (AL\ b\text{-}1)\ 100 \tag{1.2}$$

where y = future demand of power
t = points of time for which the demand is calculated
$a = \Sigma \log Y/N$; N denotes the total number of points of time.
$b = \Sigma t \log y/\Sigma t^2$
Gr = Growth rate of power consumption
AL = Antilog of b

To analyse the regional variations and compute the levels of development and electrification at district level, different units of variables were calculated into standardised values applying formula[5]:

$$SV = X\text{-}\bar{X} / SD \tag{1.3}$$

where SV = Standardised value of variable
S = actual value of the variable
$X = \Sigma X/N$, mean value for the variable
SD = Standard deviation value.

To explore the relationship between power consumption and State income in terms of State Domestic Product, quantitative measurement suggested by Karl Pearson,[6] has been taken into account, defined as follows:

$$r = \frac{\Sigma XY - \frac{\Sigma X \Sigma Y}{N}}{\sqrt{\Sigma X^2 - \frac{(\Sigma X)^2}{N}}\ \sqrt{\Sigma Y^2 - \frac{(\Sigma Y)^2}{N}}} \tag{1.4}$$

where r = coefficient of correlation,
N = number of observations,
X = State Domestic Product,
Y = Power consumption

The '*t*' test[7] has been worked-out in the following manner, so as to generalize the positive relationship between income and power of the State:

$$t = r\sqrt{\frac{n-2}{1-r^2}} \tag{1.5}$$

Energy Resources

Energy is an index of growth. For an overall development of the State it is essential to ensure adequate and sustained supply of energy to different sectors of economy both in urban and rural areas. Demand for energy is increasing at a rapid rate and the conventional sources of energy like coal and petroleum are not adequate to meet the growing demand. Rather conventional sources are depleting fast and that Hydel and Nuclear sources of energy have their own limitations. However, non-conventional sources of energy like sun, wind, biomass, agricultural residues, industrial waste, cow-dung, night-soil etc. are of renewable nature and perennial sources of energy generation. Therefore, these sources have been taken into consideration prior to the analysis of growth and consumption pattern of electricity in the State.

Solar Energy for Rajasthan

The use of solar and wind energies has been known for centuries. In early times man depended mainly on energy derived from the sun. Sun and the three sun-based sources, namely, wood, wind and waterfall had been the mainstay as energy sources for use in cooking, pumping, drying, transportation and other purposes. The advent of steam engine in the nineteenth century and the introduction of internal combustion engine in the twentieth century nearly put an end to the use and development of these energy sources. Current public awareness of the limitations of fossil fuels to supply global energy needs in the short term and longterm future has revitalized the interest in solar and wind energies.

India is richly endowed with the solar energy. On an average, it receives insolation of 5kWh per sq m per day for over 300 days per year. In Rajasthan, an abundance of insolation, equivalent to 3.4×10^{14} kWh/year is available. One per cent utilization of the same can generate 3.4×10^{12} kWh per year. In Western Rajasthan, a huge quantity of solar radiation is available. On an average, 2173.2 kWh/m² per year to 2267.6 kWh/m² per year for about 3285 hours to 3555 hours the sun-power is received in Western Rajasthan. Table 1.1 shows the details of availability of solar energy recorded at Jodhpur and Jaisalmer Meteorological stations.

TABLE 1.1: Solar Energy Available in Rajasthan

Months	Jodhpur		Jaisalmer		Insolation kWh/m	Average Temperature C
	Clear hours per month average	Insolation kWh/m	Temperature average C Thrs to 19 hrs	Average clear hrs		
January	279	144.4	19.1	285	147.3	18.9
February	269	155.8	22.8	273	159.4	22.8
March	279	233.0	28.5	290	208.9	29.6
April	300	217.0	33.6	310	218.0	34.8
May	322	233.9	36.4	330	240.2	37.6
June	384	212.0	33.1	310	218.8	36.8
July	116	156.2	—	267	184.0	—
August	198	171.9	31.9	280	173.1	33.1
September	249	183.0	28.0	273	186.2	29.7
October	313	180.6	30.5	333	197.4	31.6
November	295	147.9	25.1	310	189.2	26.0
December	280	138.6	20.6	294	149.1	21.2
Total per year	3285	2173.2	—	3555	2267.6	—
Min./yr	2984	2093.0	11.5	2480	2203.2	10.1
Max./yr	3572	2253.4	40.4	3650	2332	44.6

Source: Solar Radiation Hand Book, 1980.

The conversion of solar radiation to thermal energy represents a promising way of utilizing solar energy. A good portion of the energy required for industrial consumers and private households is in the form of thermal energy. The entire temperature range required by these target groups could be covered with available technologies of conversion of solar energy to thermal energy. Also the solar thermal energy can be converted to electricity. Solar electricity may be produced by the photovoltaic or thermodynamic process. In photovoltaic system, a semi-conductor photovoltaic cell directly convert the photon of solar energy into the electric current.

Photovoltaic system are becoming more popular and finding an increasing acceptance in rural areas. One of such applications is lighting of either houses or streets in villages or isolated places. The cost effectiveness of PV technology is being achieved by efficiently generating and utilizing the solar power. In PV technology, batteries play an important role as a source of energy storage. During the period of low insolation and at night time batteries supply the required power to the load. The PV system deployed particularly in rural remote areas, demand reliable batteries. Although suitable batteries designed for photovoltaic applications are not available, generally lead-acid batteries are being used in PV systems. Other type of batteries are also being studied and tried under field trials.

The available technologies for solar thermal conversion can be categorised into three groups ranging from 40°C low temperature applications to above 1000°C high temperature applications.[8]

Type of Application	*Type of Conversion Device*
1. Low temperature applications 40-100°C	Flat Plate Collectors
2. Medium temperature applications 100-350°C	Evacuated Tube Collectors especially concentrating parabolic trough collector
3. High temperature applications 350°C-1000°C and above temperature.	Highly concentrating Reflector systems and point focussing collectors.

Various types of flat plate collectors are available for low temperature applications. These applications include water heating, drying, distillation of water, cooking, space heating, etc. Solar water heating is one of the largest applications of solar thermal energy. Solar water heaters have been produced in large numbers in India, Japan, Australia, USA and Israel. A number of designs of solar cookers have also been evolved including solar cookers with heat storage facilities so that cooking can be done by solar energy during the non sunny hours or even during-nights.

Solar Photovoltaic Water Pumping System designed and manufactured by Rajasthan Electronics and Instruments Ltd., operated on solar energy is ideally suited for rural settlements scattered in the inaccessible areas, where conventional grid power is difficult to supply. The Solar Photovoltaic (SPv) water pumping system is designed for both agricultural and community drinking water uses. Sunlight is converted into electricity using SPV modules, which is used directly to operate a DC motor pump-set, usually mounted on top of the tube-well or open-well. The water available can be stored in a storage tank with necessary outlet point for community water distribution purposes.

Solar powered stand-alone fluorescent lights manufactured by REIL for street lighting requirements are ideal for isolated rural areas where grid power supply is difficult and transmission losses are too high. The SPV lighting system is cost effective against the conventional grid power for such areas. When it is dark and lighting is required, the electronic sensor will automatically switch on the lights and the timer switches off the light after 3/6 hours.

Solar Photovoltaic modules consist of a string of carefully selected and matched solar cells, incorporating a complex and high technology. When properly connected to an electrical or electronic system, through necessary storage or intermediate electronics, the SPV modules generate and supply electricity at the desired voltage and current. Sunlight is converted into DC electricity, when it falls on the top surfaces of the solar cells inside the SPV module, by means of direct photovoltaic conversion process. The generated electricity can either be directly used during the sunshine hours, or may be stored in storage batteries, to be used later. Such SPV modules are very useful to provide electricity where it is not available.

Photovoltaic, thermodynamic and flat plate collectors can be of greater significance, if utilized in Rajasthan where solar energy is abundantly available. On an average, one square metre of area in Rajasthan, receives 6 kWh of solar energy daily and 2200 kWh per year. Solar energy showered over Rajasthan for two days, can generate as much electricity as required for one year to the State. Central Government has already sanctioned Rs. 95 crores for installation of a 30 mW Solar Power Plant in Western Rajasthan, probably at Jodhpur.[9]

Wind Energy for Rajasthan

Wind energy is a manifestation of solar energy. It is set up and continually regenerated by a small fraction of the insolation reaching the atmosphere which, in fact, is acting as a giant heat engine fuelled by the sun. The wind is merely air in motion and exerts pressure which is proportional to square of wind speed. Wind is capable to do work and rate of this work is called 'Wind power'. The power of a wind stream at a velocity C passing through an area A is given by $P = KAC^3$. The factor K is a constant, which depends upon the density of air and on the units used for the measurements of P, A and C. If P is expressed in kilowatts, A in square metres and C in kilometres per hour, K has the value 13.7×10^{-6}. So the equation becomes $P = 13.7\times10^{-6}AC^3$. The power contained in a wind stream is 64 kilowatts if a horizontal stream of 10 metres square moves with a speed of 36 km/hr, because $P = 13.7\times10^{-6}\times10^2\times(36)^3$ = 64 kW or 48 HP.[10]

In Rajasthan the wind could be particularly useful for pumping underground water and generating electricity. Major problem in this connection is the wide variation in the speed and direction of winds coupled with the fact that there could be frequent long spells of low wind. Water can be pumped out by a wind-mill when wind blows 8 km per hour. Table 1.2 shows that during the period April to September mean number of days exceeds 20 in Jodhpur, Jaisalmer and Bikaner. Thus areas near these cities have good potential of pumping water by wind power.

TABLE 1.2: Number of Days When Mean Wind Speed is Greater Than 8 km/hour

Months	Jodhpur	Bikaner	Jaisalmer
January	13.0	1.1	18.9
February	12.7	2.5	16.1
March	17.6	5.8	22.7
April	19.8	9.7	22.9
May	27.6	19.6	28.0
June	28.8	26.1	29.6
July	28.5	25.5	30.5
August	27.1	22.3	30.3
September	20.2	17.1	27.4
October	9.4	5.0	14.2
November	6.1	0.3	7.0
December	9.7	0.7	11.2
Year	220.5	135.0	258.8

Source: Ibid., pp. 209.

Table 1.2 reveals that area near Jaisalmer is richly endowed with wind energy having 258 days of 8 km/hr mean wind velocity. Wind mill can function during each month at these stations. The period with less than ten days covers October to December in Jodhpur and only November in Jaisalmer and October to April in Bikaner. The period between May to September provides more than 20 days of high velocity.

Wind turbines could be used for electricity production in the areas of high wind velocity. Small wind electric generators could be used in farms for irrigation or supply of electricity for lighting and for running the radio or TV sets for a small community. When used for lighting the generator must be used with storage batteries that serve as a standby to ensure a constant supply. For a wind electric plant, wind velocity should be as high as 16 km/hr, which is sufficient to start a water pumping wind mill.

Wind, a form of solar energy has been recognised as a feasible alternate source of energy. It is clean, safe and replenishable source of energy but intermittent in nature. It is available with varying density depending upon wind velocity which may vary from 3 to 30 km/hr. Wind mills could be used in areas of low wind velocity and wind turbines could be installed in areas of high wind velocity. A number of wind turbines have been commissioned at Okha (Gujarat), Deogard (Maharashtra), Tuticorin (Tamil Nadu) and many more to come. It is a matter of investigation to locate the points of high and low wind velocity in Rajasthan so as to utilize cost effective and inexhaustible form of energy.

Biomass Energy for Rajasthan

Biomass is defined as unfossilized biological material and in the energy context refers to such products as animal manure, aquatic plants, agricultural crops, forestry residues and trees. It is estimated that solar energy converted through photosynthesis and stored in the form of biomass each year is ten times greater than the word's energy consumption. The total energy stored in biomass, approximately 90 per cent of which is in trees, is estimated to be equivalent to total proven fossil reserves (Hall and Moss, 1983).[11] Yet the potential of this vast supply of energy remains, for the most part, unrealized, despite the fact that nearly half of the population of the world relies on biomass for its supply of energy. The role of biomass energy in developing nations is particularly significant, providing on average 43 per cent of the total energy used, while the contribution of biomass to energy supply in the developed nations has declined rapidly since the late 1800s.[12]

Firewood and Charcoal

Forests and woodlands are an important element in the inventory of fuel resources in Rajasthan, since they are the source of firewood and charcoal which is the main item of domestic fuel consumption. Although the total amount of firewood consumed in the State is not known, but it contributes 35 to 45 per cent of the revenue assessed from forest (Table 1.3).

TABLE 1.3: Revenue Assessed from Firewood and Charcoal

(Lakhs of Rs.)

Year	Total forest revenue	Firewood/ charcoal	Per cent of total forest revenue
1977-78	538.62	224.64	41.71
1978-79	602.99	257.63	42.73
1979-80	653.41	263.06	40.26
1980-81	702.12	316.86	45.13
1981-82	858.19	328.28	44.23
1982-83	909.43	319.31	40.79
1983-84	955.04	299.85	36.38
1984-85	922.00	288.25	35.29

Source: Rajasthan Forest Statistics, 1985, Forest Deptt. Jaipur.

The total forest area of Rajasthan extends over 31151 square kilometres, which is 4.33 per cent of total forest area of the country (718973 sq km). Madhya Pradesh alone occupied about 23 per cent of total forest area of the country followed by Orissa (9.4%), Andhra Pradesh (9%), Maharashtra (7.8%), U.P. (5.8%), Karnataka (5%), Bihar (4.1%), Assam (4%) and rest of the States below 4 per cent each. The percentage of total forest area with respect to geographical area of Rajasthan accounted only 9.1 per cent and per capita forest area 0.09 hectare in the year 1983-84. Sirohi district accounted maximum (0.29) per capita forest area followed by Udaipur (0.24 ha), Bundi (0.24 ha), Kota (0.23 ha), Sawai Madhopur (0.17 ha), Chittorgarh (0.19 ha), Jhalawar (0.16 ha), Banswara (0.13 ha), Dholpur (0.11 ha), and Churu and Jodhpur districts provided negligible per capita forest area followed by Nagaur (0.01), Bharatpur (0.02), Jhunjhunu (0.03), Jalore

(0.03), Jaisalmer (0.03), Jaipur (0.03), Barmer (0.03) and rest of the districts ranging from 0.04 to 0.09 hectare per capita. In terms of percentage of total forest area with respect to geographical area, Udaipur district covered 33.31 per cent of its area followed by Sirohi (31.08%), Kota (29.23%), Bundi (26.27%), S. Madhopur (25.83%), Banswara (23.61%), Chittorgarh (22.62%), Dholpur (21.57%), Jhalawar (21.12%) and rest of the districts accounted for less than 20 per cent of their area.

A very large proportion of wood is used as firewood or charcoal. The heating value of wood is determined by measuring the quantity of heat generated by a unit weight of wood in oxygen and expressed in calories. These values for certain woods which are considered good fuels are given below:

Good Fuel Wood	*Calorific Value*
Sal	5264
Lendi	5264
Laurel	5210
Mahua	5101
Chir	5015
Jamun	4934
Casuarina	4950
Solar	4955
Semul	4885
Babul	4870
Aam	4610

The most widely accepted estimate of consumption of non-commercial fuels, and allowing for differences in thermal value, firewood accounts for almost two-thirds of the total, vegetable wastes for about 20 per cent, and cowdung for about 15 per cent.[13] Since vegetable wastes are mainly derived from crop residues, the available quantities largely depend on the amounts harvested of the crops concerned. Hence total cropped area and total forest area of a region is of greater significance while considering firewood potentiality (Table 1.4).

Table 1.4 shows that more then 60 per cent area of the State is covered by crops and forest, which provides about 85 per cent of State's non-commercial fuels. A serious consequence of the extensive use of wood as an energy source is deforestation. This has wide ranging effects, including the loss of top soil, erosion, silting of dams and streams, increased flooding and possible climatic changes. The problem can be remedied through reforestation and replantation schemes which are not well developed in Rajasthan.

TABLE 1.4: Firewood Potential Area (sq km)

Year	Cropped area	Per cent of total	Forest area	Per cent of total
1977-78	—	—	34484	10.08
1978-79	174952.00	51.12	34913	10.20
1979-80	163710.01	47.83	30656	8.96
1980-81	173496.34	50.69	30439	8.89
1981-82	185967.61	54.33	30828	9.01
1982-83	183948.05	53.74	31130	9.09
1983-84	—	—	31151	9.10

Source: Statistical Abstract 1983 and Rajasthan Forest Statistics 1985.

Biogas Plants in Rajasthan

A renewable energy source like biogas is expected to have a promising future in Rajasthan, where total livestock density is (145 per sq/km) greater than the population density (100). According to 1983 Statistical Abstract of Rajasthan, the livestock population is about 50 million animal out of which cattle and buffaloes account for 19.51 million. With an average out-turn of 3 kg dry dung per animal per day (10 kg of wet dung), the annual yield can be estimated to be 16.024 million tonnes equivalent to 8000 million kW electricity on the basis of assumptions used in Table 1.5.

TABLE 1.5: Assumptions used for Biogas Power Generation

Item	Units	Tyner's value	Rajasthan
1. Dry dung/animal/day	kg	3	3
2. No. of animals in Rajasthan	No.	300	1,95,11,516
3. Dry dung/Rajasthan/day	kg	900	5,85,34,548
4. Collection efficiency	%	75	75
5. Usable dry dung/Raj./day	kg	675	4,39,00,911
6. Biogas yield/kg dry dung	cu/ft	11	11
7. Energy content/cu.ft. of biogas	BTU	620	620
8. Conversion factor	kWh/BTU	3413	3413
9. Power generation efficiency	%	25	25
10. Maximum power generation/day	kWh	337	2,19,17,936

Table 1.5 provides the yield assumptions used by Wallace E. Tyner[14] in his biogas analysis. On the basis of Tyner's assumptions, maximum power generation capacity from animal-dung in Rajasthan, has been computed. Table reveals that 19.5 million cattle and buffaloes provide 43.9 million kilogram usable dry dung per day at 75 per cent collection efficiency. According to Tyner's assumptions that 11 cubic feet per kilogram of dry dung and a gas energy content of 620 British Thermal Units, multiplying the daily yield of usable dry dung (43.9 million kg) by the biogas yield (11 cu/ft) and by the energy content (620 BTU) Rajasthan gets 2,99,398 BTU of energy per day. With a power generation efficiency of 25 per cent and conversion factor 3413 kWh/BTU, 21.92 million kWh of power would be available per day in Rajasthan, which is sufficient to illuminate streets and roads of 201 towns and cities of Rajasthan for one year. Moreover, 8000 mkWh annual availability of power from animal dung is sufficient for two years for entire Rajasthan. Availability of fertilizer is a matter of further investigation.

It seems very attractive to have a huge quantity of power from animal dung. But the major problem with biogas based power generation lies in the transformation of the biogas energy into electrical energy. Small scale generators are not efficient convertors of energy. However, use of the biogas energy directly as fuel is more attractive. Biogas could be used both for heat and light. The energy yield from biogas is greater than the energy yield obtained from directly burning the dung. The energy content of dried dung is about 14000 BTU/kg. Burning efficiency of dung cakes is much lower than biogas burning efficiency, and fertilizer value is lost when the dung is burnt. With the use of biogas for cooking, heating and lighting, significant energy savings in other sources would be achieved and a good fertile manure would be obtained.

TABLE 1.6: Cost and Capacity of Biogas Plants

Size of Biogas Cubic Metre	Plant Cubic feet	Number of animals	Cost of plant (Rupees)	Subsidy w.e.f. 1-4-87	Meals can be prepared for No. of persons
2	70	2- 3	4200	2940	8-10
3	105	3- 4	5250	3660	10-12
4	140	4- 6	5800	4390	12-15
6	210	6-10	7350	5350	15-20
8	280	12-15	9400	5900	20-30
10	350	16-20	10900	5900	40-50
15	525	25-30	17750	6460	60-70

Source: Biogas Cell, special scheme and IRDP Deptt. Secretariat, Jaipur.

Table 1.6 shows that a biogas plant of 2 cu m capacity can be installed at the cost of Rs. 1,260 only, which can provide sufficient gas for cooking food for 8-10 persons and can be operated with the dung obtained from 2-3 animals. Due to growing importance of renewable sources of energy the Government has increased the amount of subsidy for setting up of biogas plants. As per Biogas Cell, 22,845 biogas plants have been installed so far as against potentiality of 12 million plants of 3 cu m gas per plant per day capacity (Table 1.7).

TABLE 1.7: **Livestock and Biogas Plants in Rajasthan**

Districts	Livestock (millions)	Density (sq km)	Probability Biogas Plants (in '000) (50% efficiency)	Plants installed so far
1. Ajmer	1.986	234	993	1143
2. Alwar	1.654	197	827	891
3. Banswara	1.025	204	512	336
4. Barmer	3.184	112	1592	185
5. Bharatpur	0.993	179	496	853
6. Bhilwara	2.685	257	1342	1437
7. Bikaner	2.075	76	1037	626
8. Bundi	0.969	175	484	545
9. Chittor	1.845	170	922	635
10. Churu	2.043	121	1021	750
11. Dholpur	0.454	150	227	225
12. Dungarpur	1.111	295	555	406
13. Jaipur	3.115	221	1557	831
14. Jaisalmer	1.631	42	815	171
15. Jalore	1.476	139	738	464
16. Jhalawar	1.003	161	501	432
17. Jhunjhunu	1.176	198	588	816
18. Jodhpur	2.666	117	1333	1081
19. Kota	1.460	117	730	781
20. Nagor	3.037	171	1513	650
21. Pali	2.012	162	1006	910
22. S. Madhopur	1.791	170	895	1250
23. Sikar	1.759	228	879	423
24. Sirohi	0.762	148	381	404
25. Sri Ganganagar	2.178	106	1089	2277
26. Tonk	1.473	205	736	450
27. Udaipur	3.945	228	1972	3872
Total	49.508	145	24754	22845

Nuclear Energy for Rajasthan

There was no specific allocation in the First Plan to nuclear energy development. By the beginning of the Second Plan, India was committed to the development of her atomic energy raw materials and implementation of atomic power generating facilities. An atomic reactor at Trombay was scheduled for completion in the Second Plan. A number of projects were planned for exploration, extraction, or processing of nuclear raw materials. The Third Plan included a provision for establishing a nuclear power plant. Rs. 51 crores was allocated to constructing the atomic power plant, and Rs. 35 crores to the Department of Atomic Energy for research. Investment in nuclear energy continued in the Fourth Plan with planned total of Rs. 64.3 crores. During the Fifth Plan 705 million kW of nuclear generating capacity was scheduled to be completed along with a 40 megawatt Fast Breeder Thermal Reactor. India is richly endowed with reserves of thorium which can be used as a fuel in the breeder reactors now being developed. India's 450,000 tons of thorium constitute the worlds largest reserves. A number of uranium deposits have been located in Bihar, Rajasthan and Madras. It is estimated that there are 2.8 million tonnes of ore of grade 0.076 and 0.1 per cent of U_3O_8. The total amount of uranium is about 2000 tonnes which will yield 10,000 mW/day per ton sufficient to provide one million kW of nuclear power for 20 years. Uranium deposits near Udaipur in Rajasthan may prove worth developing, though the uranium concentration is expected to be considerably lower. Prospecting and exploration work for uranium is being carried out in a number of different regions under the Direction of the Department of Atomic Energy in collaboration with other government agencies.

Rajasthan Atomic Power Station comprises two units of 200 mW each. The first unit became critical during 1972 and the first power was delivered during February 1973. This project has been taken up by the Department of Atomic Energy, Government of India. It was expected that the successful commissioning of this station would go a long way in mitigating the power shortage in the State, but the shortfall of power is still experienced, due to failure of power generation in its full swing. Improvements in fuel and plant technology in the present reactors need a greater emphasis in developing the atomic power plant.

Table 1.8 shows that the atomic energy shared 28 per cent of total availability in Rajasthan in 1977, the maximum share attained so far, since the installation of the Atomic Power Plant. Whereas, only 4.84 per cent atomic power could be shared in 1978 due to certain mishandling. In the year 1981, 22 per cent share was obtained once again increasing the atomic share after many mishaps. It declined to 7.9 per cent in 1983 and increased to 17.26 per cent in 1986. The fluctuating availability of atomic power create uncertainty of adequate supply of power in the State, alike the monsoons which tend to fluctuate the hydroelectric generation. It can be emphasized here that the supply of power in Rajasthan should be stabilized by attaining improved level of technology and harnessing its power potential sources like running water, wind, insolation, fossil, biomass and so on.

TABLE 1.8: Atomic energy for Rajasthan (RAPP)

Year	Atomic mkWh	Total availability mkWh	Percentage of total
1974	421.133	2493.843	16.88
1975	658.674	2703.732	24.36
1976	468.852	3011.170	15.57
1977	954.973	3404.152	28.05
1978	155.770	3220.739	4.84
1979	389.802	4165.773	9.36
1980	1001.847	4878.743	20.53
1981	1050.984	4717.739	22.28
1982	870.015	4819.754	18.05
1983	391.605	4938.316	7.93
1984	967.269	6013.558	16.08
1985	841.200	6241.888	13.47
1986	1082.823	6274.332	17.26
1987	1500	6780	22.12
1988	1529	7589	20.15
1989	1578	8916	17.69
1990	1653	9943	16.62

Source: Annual Statistical Reports of RSEB.

NOTES

1. *Some Facts about Rajasthan, 1986*; Directorate of Economics and Statistics, Jaipur.
2. Statistical Abstract, Rajasthan 1984, Directorate of Eco. and Statistics, Jaipur.
3. *Budget Study, 1987-88*, (*Ibid*), pp.106-107.

4. Pillai, pp. (1984) "Regional Power Scenario in 2001 AD: case of Kerala" in *Indian journal of Regional Science*, Vol. XVI, No. 1, pp.46-53.
5. John Silk, (1979). "Statistical concept in Geography", George Allen and Unwin, London, pp. 86.
6. Aslam Mahmood, 1977, "Statistical methods in Geographical Studies", pp.49-60.
7. Hammond, R. and McCullagh, P.S., 1977, "Quantitative Techniques in Geography: An Introduction", Clarendon Press, Oxford, pp.199.
8. Energy Options for 90's, National Solar Energy Convention of the Solar Energy Society of India, Dec. 2-4, 1987. IIT, New Delhi.
9. *Rajasthan Patrika*, January 24, 1988.
10. Garg, H.P. and Kaushik, N.D., (1983). "Solar and Wind Energy Utilization" in *Desert Resources and Technology*, Vol. I, pp.179-220.
11. Hall, D. and Moss, P., (1983). Biomass for energy in developing countries, *Geo-Journal*, 7, 5-14.
12. Cocklin, C.; Lonergan and Clarke, (1985). Forest Energy plantations: An International Perspective, *Geoforum*, Vol. 16, No. 3, pp.257-264.
13. Henderson, P.D., (1975), *India: The Energy Sector*, Oxford University Press, pp.23-24.
14. Tyner, E. Wallace, (1978). *Energy Resources and Economic Development in India*, Martinus Nijhoff Social Sciences Division London/Boston, pp.111-124.

2

ENERGY NETWORK PATTERN IN RAJASTHAN

THE INDUSTRIAL and agricultural revolutions, growing transportation and communication network, and the development of other branches of economy puts forward an ever growing demand for energy.

Of all now known sources of energy, electricity is the most convenient for use in economy. It can be quickly and efficiently transmitted over long distances, and easily converted to other forms of energy. The electrical power is transmitted in large quantities from where it is cheaply and conveniently produced to somewhere else, many kilometres away where it can be used to advantage. All this together with its availability for immediate use makes it indispensable in most production processes of the modern community. To meet the demand of energy for various sectors of economy, large power systems are being constructed and modified to cover sizeable regions embracing many cities and towns, factories and farms, shops and houses and so on. Such powerful systems of electric power are hardly possible without construction of economically effective transmission lines used to convey electric power, in particular over long distances. The lines are constantly modified to improve their construction, equipment, reliability and economy.

The more powerful the power plant, the larger the area under its service. Therefore, the transmission of electric energy from the power station to the consumption centres is of great significance, the problem being solved by installing transmission lines. A transmission network essentially comprises aerial (overhead) high voltage transmission lines which deliver bulk power from the generating stations to the sub-stations and on to the switchgear devices of the consumers. Low-voltage underground cable lines are used to deliver the electric power directly to the receiving devices of the consumers. Sometimes, when transmission lines must traverse more densely populated areas or localities where space is of premium, high voltage cable systems are in use.

At present, several power stations (Rajasthan Atomic Power Plant, Chambal Hydraulic Power Plant and Thermal Power Plant), interconnected by transmission lines and operating into a common network form an electric power system. Interconnection of all units of the system makes possible great economies and efficiency of performance of the system as a whole. To reduce the electric power loss, it is good practice to decrease current and increase the voltage. To increase the transmission voltage, step-up substations are built at the generating stations. The power is then transmitted over high-voltage transmission lines to step-down substations built at considerable distances in the area of supply (Fig 2.1). There may be several steps up and down in a power system. An electric power system is meant a complex of power structures including power stations, transmission lines, transformer substations and continuous process of power generation and distribution among its consumers. Hence the study of energy net-work pattern is essential while examining the energy problem of a region.

Growth of Energy Network in Rajasthan

Table 2.1 pertinent to EHT and H.T. transmission lines, reveals plan-wise growth of 11 kV and above lines in Rajasthan. At the end of First Five Year Plan in 1955-56 a total network of lines were of the order of 330 circuit km only, sharing 41.5 per cent for 33 kV and 58.5 per cent for 11 kV transmission lines. Above 33 kV lines were non-existent. Figure 2.2 illustrates the network as on March 1986.

At the end of Second Five Year Plan the total network made a tremendous growth of 423.3 per cent over the plan period, making a share of 18.6 per cent, 13.4 per cent, 45.5 per cent and 22.5 per cent for 132 kV, 66 kV, 33 kV and 11 kV transmission lines respectively. In the year 1965-66, ending Third Five Year Plan, an aggregate network of 10,525 circuit km, consisting of 1148 (10.9%) km 132 kV, 344 (3.3%) km 66 kV, 3857 (37%) km 33 kV and 5176 (49.2%) km 11 kV lines, again made an impressive increase of 509.4 per cent over the plan period. The energy supply network including 919 circuit km of the length of 220 kV lines, rose to 33260 circuit km making a growth of 113 per cent over the previous figure by the end of Fourth Five Year Plan. Another 16250 circuit kilometres were added to the supply system of the State during the period of Fifth Five Year Plan making an increase of 48.85 per cent over the previous figure.

At the end of Sixth Plan Period the length of energy supply system was of the order of 96831 circuit kilometres. It is important to note that 74.4 per cent of the total length of the network was accounted by 11 kV lines and remaining 25.6 per cent by 33 kV, 66 kV, 132 kV ha and 220 kV systems. Obviously, the increasing rural-electrification is responsible for the rapid growth of 11 kV transmission system. Similarly, it is of greater significance to note that the increasing length of low voltage transmission-lines, has also increased the power losses in supply system (Fig. 2.5).

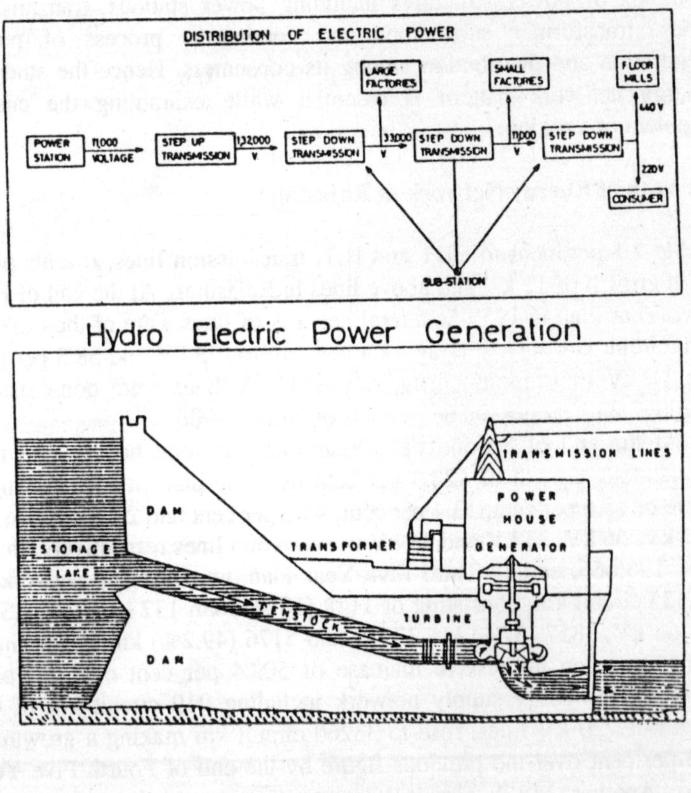

FIG. 2.1

TABLE 2.1: Plan-wise Growth of Energy Network Transmission

End of Plan	Transmitting Voltage kV/Length in Circuit km										Total
	220 kV	%	132 kV	%	66 kV	%	33 kV	%	11 kV	%	
I	—	—	—	—	—	—	137	41.5	193	58.5	330
II	—	—	321	18.6	232	13.4	785	45.5	389	22.5	1727
III	—	—	1148	10.9	344	3.3	3857	36.6	5176	49.2	10525
(3)	115	0.7	1753	11.2	412	2.6	5028	32.3	8307	53.2	15615
IV	919	2.8	2376	7.1	415	1.2	8691	26.2	20859	62.7	33260
V	1250	2.5	3716	7.5	415	0.8	10877	22.0	33252	67.2	49510
(4)	1389	2.1	4047	6.1	415	0.6	12970	19.4	48079	71.8	66927
VI	2666	2.7	5987	6.2	303	0.3	15876	16.4	71999	74.4	96831
VII	4200	3.3	7500	5.8	303	0.2	19750	15.4	96500	75.3	128253
VIII	5600	3.5	9200	5.8	300	0.2	23500	14.8	121000	75.7	159748
IX	7000	3.7	10950	5.7	300	0.2	27250	14.2	146000	76.2	191500

POWER MAP OF RAJASTHAN
(As on 31st March 1986)

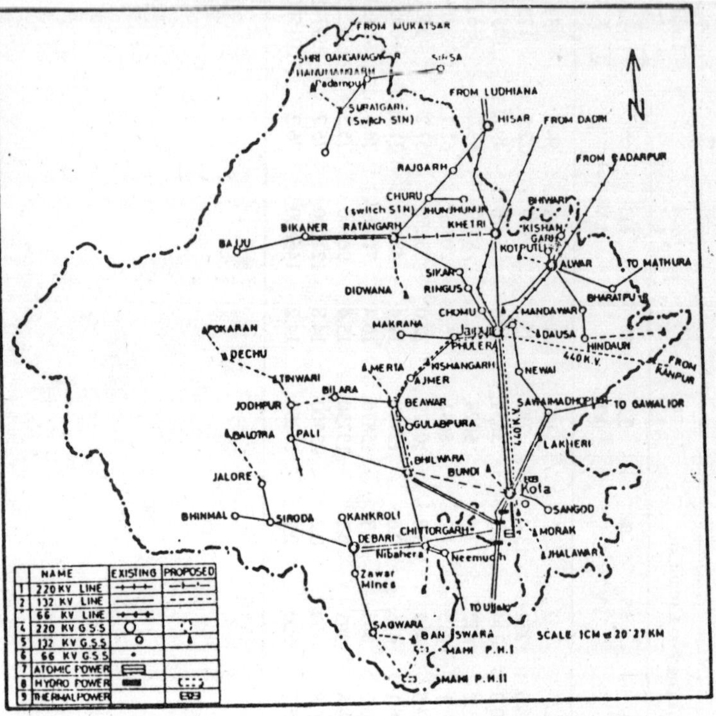

FIG. 2.2

The growth patterns of power supply network tend to further increase in low voltage supply system and decrease in high voltage systems which is an indicator of higher losses in supply system. To decrease the transmission losses it is necessary to increase the length of high voltage supply systems.

Integrated Operation of Power Stations

An interconnection between power generating centres or power systems helps to coordinate the generating plants of adjacent regions and beyond, providing mutual power supply exchange from one system to another between the surplus and deficit areas. The nation-wide extension of high voltage interconnections can have an economic effect much beyond the efficient use of plant and equipment and also reduce the amount of investment and decrease the transmission-losses. The recent trends in the transmission system is towards EHT transmission lines. The level has now successfully reached 220 kV accounting 2666 circuit km in 1985 which was only 115 km in 1969. A 400 kV sub-station is working at Jaipur since December 1986 getting power from Singrauli for Rajasthan by Kanpur-Agra-Jaipur 400 kV line and plans are now envisaged to build and augment 380 kV and 440 kV lines to the areas of higher quantum of power utilisation. A 500 kV transmission line can transmit a given quantity of power more than twice as far as can a 345 kV line and 5 or more times as far as can a 230 kV line. A 150 miles 230 kV line and a 500 mile 345 kV line have about the same transmission capacity.* The advantage of EHT lines advocates an immediate necessity in Rajasthan where Power Generation Plants are concentrated in one corner.

Distribution of Transformers

The total number of transformers at the end of March 1985, were 48,176 with their aggregate installed capacity of 99,68,108 kVA. The figure includes step-up and step-down above and below 550 voltage transformers. To increase the transmission voltage, step-up sub-stations are built at the generating stations. The power is then transmitted over high-voltage transmission line to step-down sub-stations built at varying distances in the areas of power-consumption.

District-wise distribution of transformers and their installed capacity with their percentage of total, area-covered and person served by one transformer and average capacity of a transformer have been calculated. It is important to consider that 1.27 per cent of the total population of Jaisalmer is served by one transformer, where the density of population is merely six persons per square kilometre. While, in Jaipur, only 0.02 per cent persons served by a transformer, where the

* Demand for Energy in India — National Council of Applied Economic Research, New Delhi, p. 103.

density is 242 persons per square kilometer. It is interesting to contrast the two districts of minimum and maximum population density. Though these districts are not comparable in any respect, we may postulate a hypothesis that much more persons are served by a transformer in a sparsely populated area than that of a densely populous area. Diversified socio-economic activities tend to decrease the number of persons served by a transformer, roughly in the eastern districts of Rajasthan. Whereas primitive type of economic-activities increase the number of persons served by a transformer mainly in the Thar part of the State.

Chorology of Energy Network

To analyse and evaluate the district-wise distribution pattern of energy network 33 kV and 11 kV transmission lines and the low voltage power supply lines have been taken into consideration. District-wise percentage has been calculated to draw network maps so as to compare one district from the other in view of the share in a particular voltage line. Similarly, the district-wise percentage of the total power-supply system is calculated to identify the network intensity. Further a chart is prepared to illustrate the district variation according to percentage of a particular network system, and maps are prepared on the basis of this illustration (Table 2.2)

Table 2.2 pertaining energy network data as on March 1985, reveals that Jaipur district stood first having 8.9 per cent of the total 33 kV transmission lines followed by Shri Ganganagar (6.5%), Nagore (6.1%), Udaipur (5.97%) and Jodhpur district (5.5%). The minimum length of the system was shared by Jaisalmer district accounting only 0.76 per cent. Fourteen districts remained below the State average (3.7 percentage) while thirteen above the average. Table 2.3 and Fig. 2.3 exhibit the chorology of the network.

Intensity of Energy Network

The intensity of energy network calculated in km/sq km in Table 2.2 and illustrated in Fig. 2.4 shows that nine districts namely, Banswara, Bundi, Dungarpur, Jalor, Jhalawar, Kota, Nagor, Sawai Madhopur and Udaipur were the (medium level) average districts in terms of intensity of energy network ranging between 0.5 to 0.75 km per sq km. Ten districts remained above the State-average and seven districts below the average. Alwar, Jaipur, Jhunjhunu and Sikar districts accounted for (Very High Level) more than one km circuit transmission network per sq km, while Barmer, Bikaner and Jaisalmer remained below 0.25 km/sq km, the very Low Level of intensity. Six districts namely, Ajmer, Bharatpur, Bhilwara, Chittorgarh, Pali and Sirohi were categorised as High level districts whereas Churu, Jodhpur, Sri Ganganagar and Tonk district were grouped in Low Level category of intensity of energy network developed till March 1985.

TABLE 2.2: District-wise Energy Network Till March, 1985 (in percentage of the system)

District	33 kV	11 kV	DL	Total	Intensity km/sq km
1. Ajmer	2.00	3.53	3.93	3.62	0.804
2. Alwar	4.63	4.52	7.49	6.13	1.378
3. Banswara	1.70	1.88	1.21	1.50	0.563
4. Barmer	4.80	2.58	1.17	2.00	0.133
5. Bharatpur	1.82	2.81	2.90	2.78	0.836
6. Bhilwara	4.21	4.66	4.02	4.28	0.771
7. Bikaner	4.25	3.66	1.08	2.32	0.160
8. Bundi	1.35	1.89	1.34	1.53	0.521
9. Chittorgarh	2.96	4.38	5.38	4.83	0.834
10. Churu	3.22	2.95	1.31	2.09	0.234
11. Dholpur	1.75	0.85	0.66	0.82	+ in Bh.
12. Dungarpur	1.59	1.59	1.01	1.28	0.639
13. Jaipur	8.90	9.03	15.92	12.73	1.705
14. Jalore	3.27	3.84	3.63	3.68	0.652
15. Jaisalmer	0.76	0.52	0.97	0.31	0.015
16. Jhunjhunu	4.88	4.29	6.82	5.70	1.812
17. Jhalawar	2.10	2.06	1.92	1.99	0.602
18. Jodhpur	5.52	6.06	3.51	4.64	0.382
19. Kota	3.94	3.96	3.04	3.46	0.525
20. Nagor	6.08	6.44	4.62	5.43	0.578
21. Pali	4.76	5.38	4.86	5.05	0.768
22. S. Madhopur	3.78	3.08	3.80	3.52	0.630
23. Sikar	4.61	5.76	8.25	7.01	1.708
24. Sirohi	2.71	2.21	2.25	2.27	0.832
25. Sri Ganga-Nagar	6.46	4.65	2.70	3.75	0.342
26. Tonk	1.98	2.02	1.62	1.80	0.471
27. Udaipur	5.97	5.40	5.49	5.50	0.599
Total km	15116	71746	101546	188408	0.550

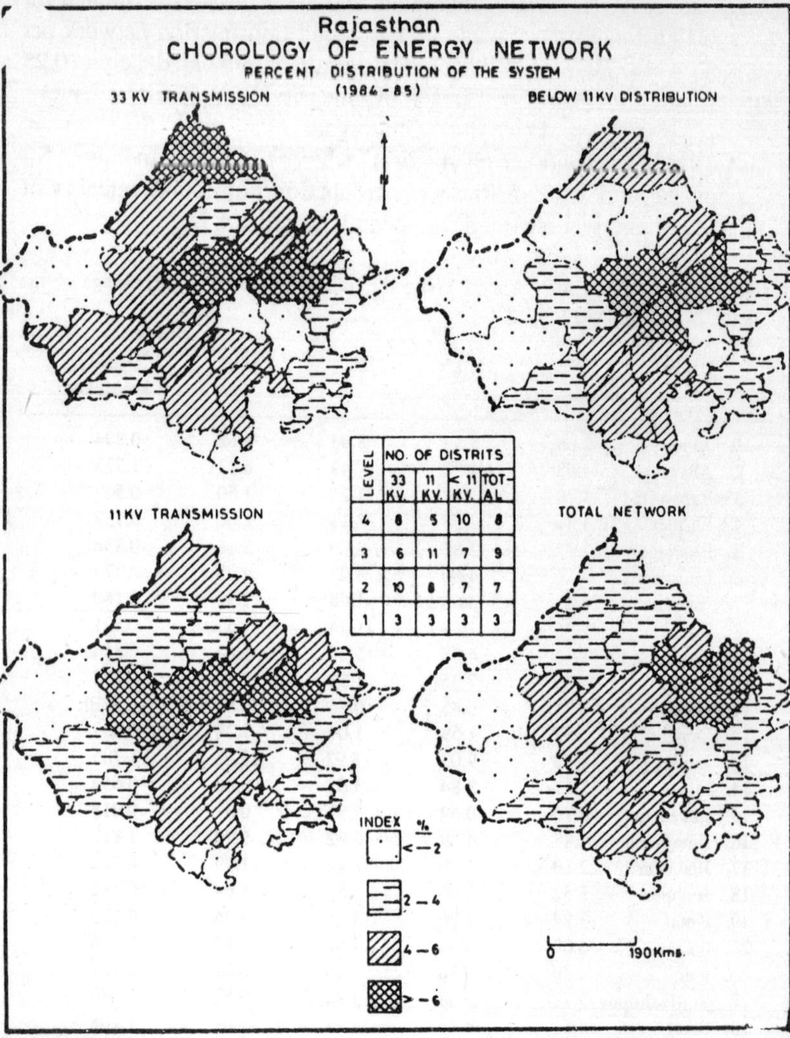

Rajasthan
CHOROLOGY OF ENERGY NETWORK
PERCENT DISTRIBUTION OF THE SYSTEM
(1984-85)
33 KV TRANSMISSION
BELOW 11 KV DISTRIBUTION
N
11 KV TRANSMISSION
TOTAL NETWORK
LEVEL
NO. OF DISTRITS
33 KV.
11 KV.
< 11 KV.
TOT-AL
4 8 5 10 8
3 6 11 7 9
2 10 8 7 7
1 3 3 3 3
INDEX %
< — 2
2 — 4
4 — 6
> — 6
0
190 Kms.

FIG. 2.3

TABLE 2.3: Chorology of Energy Network (1985)

System Category	Percentage	No. of districts	Name of Districts
33 kV	< 2	8	Ajmer, Banswara, Bharatpur, Bundi, Dholpur, Dungarpur, Jaisalmer, Tonk
	2-4	6	Churu, Jalor, Jhalawar, Kota, S. Madhopur, Sirohi.
	4-6	10	Udaipur, Sikar, Pali, Jodhpur, Jhunjhunu, Bikaner, Bhilwara, Barmer, Alwar, Chittor.
	> 6	3	Jaipur, Sri Ganganagar, Nagor
11 kV	< 2	5	Banswara, Bundi, Dholpur, Dungarpur, Jaisalmer
	2-4	11	Ajmer, Barmer, Bharatpur, Bikaner, Churu, Jalor, Kota, s. Madhopur, Sirohi, Tonk, Jhalawar.
	4-6	8	Alwar, Bhilwara, Chittor, Jhunjhunu, Pali, Sikar, Ganga Nagar, Udaipur.
	> 6	3	Jaipur, Nagor, Jodhpur
D.L. Below 11 kV	< 2	10	Banswara, Barmer, Bikaner, Bundi, Churu, Dholpur, Dungarpur, Jaisalmer, Jhalawar, Tonk
	4-6	7	Alwar, Bharatpur, Jalor, Jodhpur, Kota, Sawai Madhopur, Sirohi
	4-6	7	Bhilwara, Chittor, Jhunjhunu, Pali, Sikar, Sri Ganganagar, Udaipur
	> 6	3	Jaipur, Nagaur, Ajmer
Total Network	< 2	8	Banswara, Bundi, Dhaulpur, Dungarpur, Jaisalmer, Tonk, Jhalawar, Barmer
	2-4	9	Ajmer, Bharatpur, Bikaner, Churu, Jalor, Kota, S. Madhopur, Sirohi, S. Ganganagar.
	4-6	7	Chittor Garh, Jhunjhunu, Jodhpur, Nagor, Pali, Udaipur, Bhilwara
	> 6	3	Alwar, Jaipur, Sikar

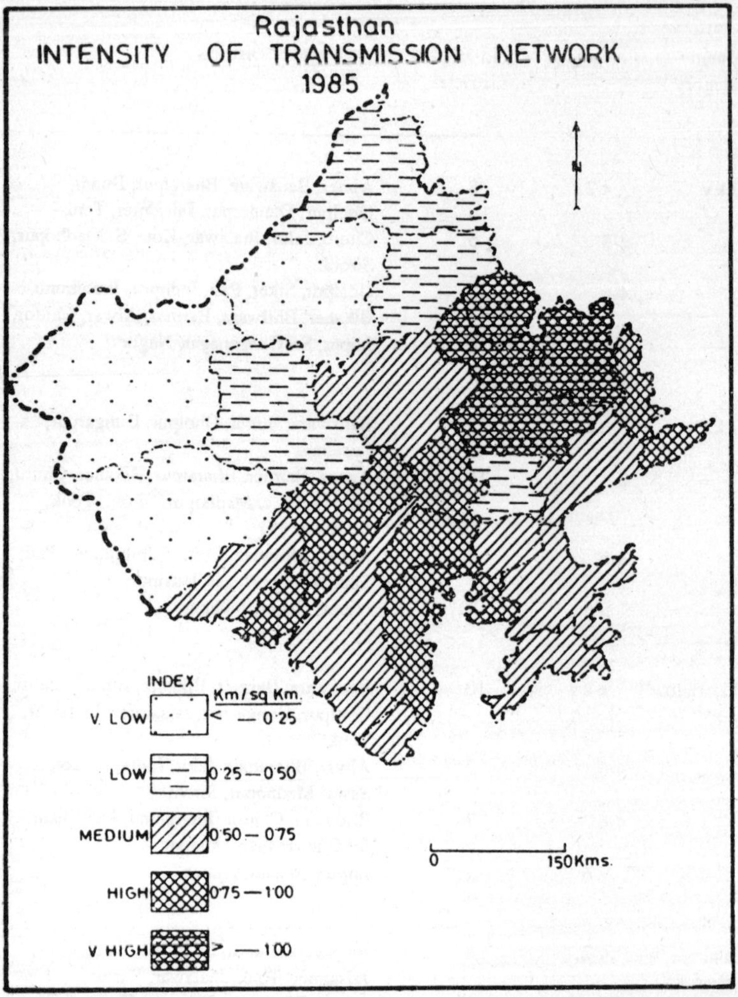
Rajasthan
INTENSITY OF TRANSMISSION NETWORK
1985
N
INDEX
Km/sq Km.
V. LOW < — 0·25
LOW 0·25 — 0·50
MEDIUM 0·50 — 0·75
HIGH 0·75 — 1·00
V HIGH > — 1·00
0
150Kms.

FIG. 2.4

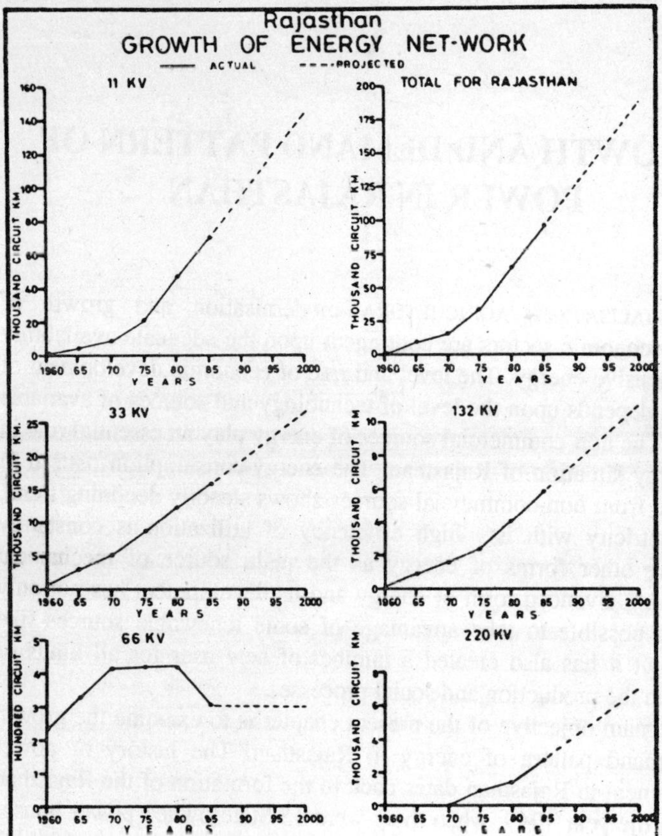
Rajasthan
GROWTH OF ENERGY NET-WORK
ACTUAL
PROJECTED
11 KV
TOTAL FOR RAJASTHAN
33 KV
132 KV
66 KV
220 KV
THOUSAND CIRCUIT KM.
HUNDRED CIRCUIT KM
YEARS

FIG. 2.5

3

GROWTH AND DEMAND PATTERN OF POWER IN RAJASTHAN

INDUSTRIALISATION, AGRICULTURAL-modernisation and growth of various economic sectors are contingent upon the adequate availability of inexpensive energy. The level and rate of economic development of a region depends upon the level of technology and sources of available energy. The non-commercial sources of energy play an essential role in the energy situation of Rajasthan. The energy-consumption pattern in the State from non-commercial sources shows steadily declining trend. The electricity with its high efficiency of utilization is constantly replacing other forms of energy as the main source of mechanical power. An advanced form of energy and its development has not only made is possible to take advantage of some renewable sources like water, but it has also created a number of new uses for all kinds of energy in the production and social processes.

The main objective of the present chapter is to examine the growth and demand pattern of energy in Rajasthan. The history of power development in Rajasthan dates back to the formation of the Rajasthan State in the year 1949, when there were 15 State owned power houses with an installed capacity of only 30.27 mW. There was no extra high voltage transmission system in the State. Sub-transmission system comprised of 136 km of 33 kV lines and 192 km of 11kV lines. The power sector in Rajasthan developed only after the formation of the Rajasthan State Electricity Board on 1 July, 1957. The installed capacity of the order of 1713.16 mW had been attained at the end of March 1985 as against 30.21 mW at the time of formation of the State. Today, approximately 30 per cent of the State Plan outplay is allocated to power sector, the major areas being power generation, transmission, sub-transmission and distribution of power in Rajasthan.

The principal sources of power supply in Rajasthan, are Inter-State projects namely Bhakra-Beas Complex, Chambal-Satpura Complex and Central Sector power stations like Rajasthan Atomic Power Plant in Kota and Singrauli-Super Thermal Power in MP. Kota Thermal Power Station commissioned in 1983 is the only station under direct administrative and operational control of Rajasthan. Even after much exploitation of State's known hydel potential the supply of electric power has not been able to cope pace with the growing demand. It was therefore, imperative to undertake the development of Thermal power. Kota Thermal Project Stage-I which envisages installation of two generating units of 110 mW each is the first major beginning towards this goal. This is followed by Kota Stage-II project under which work on installation of two generating units of 210 mW each is on going. To bridge the further gap between demand and availability and keeping in view that hydel potential within State is meagre many more thermal projects big, medium and small would have to be established in the State.

The Government of India sanctioned installation of the thermal plant at Kota, comprising of 2×110 mW units under stage I in September 1976 and augmentation of the above capacity by 2×210 mW Units in October 1980 under stage-II. The present estimated cost of Stages I and II are Rs. 143 crores and Rs. 230 crores respectively. The site for the Thermal Power Station at Kota was selected considering the availability of water in abundance from the Kota Barrage, nearness of Broad-gauge Railway line, proximity to load centre and inter-connection with the Nuclear Power Station and Hydro-stations through 220 kV line and 132 kV transmission lines. Thus it helped in stabilising the system by reducing the transmission losses and costs. The site has other added advantage of providing good foundation strata, availability of adequate area for ash disposal and construction of staff colony without displacing any population and also having good communication linkages with other parts of the region.

In addition to Kota Thermal Power Plant there are 22 State owned Power Houses of an installed capacity of 147.6 thousand kW. Table 3A.1 shows the number of Power Houses with their rated and de-rated capacity during 1981-82. All these Power Houses were running at a loss for several years. The plant and machinery in most cases were extremely old and inefficient and in several cases had even outlived their lives. Their continued operation resulted in excessive cost of generation and with the rates for supply of power far below the cost of generation and supply, the Power Houses could not make any profit. The situation is still worst today even after renovation and augmentation of these Power Houses.

TABLE 3A.1: State-owned Power Houses

Towns	Number of Power Houses	Installed Capacity kW	De-rated Capacity kW
1. Alwar	1	2,000	1,600
2. Banswara	1	424	200
3. Bharatpur	1	4,156	3,125
4. Bikaner	1	620	572
5. Barmer	1	2,000	450
6. Dholpur	1	104	50
7. Jaipur	2	10,000	10,000
8. Jaisalmer	1	1,280	100
9. Jodhpur	2	10,000	8,100
10. Kushalgarh	1	208	125
11. Malpura	1	125	95
12. Phalodi	1	500	150
13. Pokaran	1	250	100
14. Tonk	1	80	40
15. Aburoad	1	866	505
16. Mt. Abu	1	657	288
17. Udaipur	1	60	50
18. Rana Pratap Sagar	1	300	200
19. Jawahar Sagar	1	948	550
20. Kota Thermal	1	110,000	110,000
Total	22	147,578	136,300

Source : RSEB, Jaipur.

3A. Progress in Allocation of Power

Table 3A.2 shows the source-wise progress in installed capacity and allocation of power to the State of Rajasthan. The Rajasthan State Electricity Board was constituted with effect from the 1st July, 1957. The objective of this enactment was coordinated development and rationalisation of production and supply of electricity on a regional basis in the most efficient and economical way. With the formation of the RSEB in 1957 all the electricity undertakings functioning under the Electrical and Mechanical Department of the Government were transferred to the Board.

The power-development of any State or region is the first pre-requisite for its overall development. Adequate availability of electric power is the greatest incentive for industrial as well as agricultural growth of a region. It is in this context, that the power-development in Rajasthan assumes special importance. A review of the pre-independence period in Rajasthan indicates that the State was lagging far behind the rest of the country as far as power development was concerned. Even at the beginning of the First Five Year Plan there were only 42 electrified localities.

TABLE 3A.2: Progress of Power Availability in Rajasthan

Sl. No.	Power Station	Rajasthan 1968-69	Share/Allocation (mW) 1979-80	1985-86
1.	Rajasthan Atomic Power Station	—	220.00	440.00
2.	Kota Thermal Power Station	—	—	220.00
3.	Chambal Project	122.00	193.00	193.00
4.	Bhakra-Nangal Project	165.06	183.32	206.15
5.	Pong (Beas Project Unit II)	—	140.40	210.60
6.	Dehar (Beas Project Unit I)	—	132.00	198.00
7.	Satpura Thermal Power Station	100.00	125.00	125.00
8.	Singrauli Thermal Power Station	—	—	123.53
9.	Local Power Stations	85.77	43.14	80.53
		472.83	1036.86	1796.81

After Independence, all development activities including those in the power sector, were initiated in a planned manner. Much progress could not however be made during the First Five Year Plan, as the same was finalised very late due to the pre-occupation of the administrative machinery with the problems arising out of integration of the various princely States. However, the installed capacity increased from 13.271 mW to 34.9 mW by the end of First Five Year Plan, and the number of electrified localities also increased to 66.

Substantial progress, in respect of power development in the State was achieved during the Second Five Year Plan. The generating stations envisaged under first stage of the Bhakra Nangal Project, as well as Chambal Project were commissioned during this period. The installed generating capacity in the State also increased from 34.9 mW to 134.568 mW by the end of the Second Five Year Plan, accounting 58 mW from local steam and oil generation, 42 mW from Bhakra Nangal Project and rest of the 34.5 mW from Gandhi Sagar Hydro Electric Project.

During the Third Five Year Plan, it was envisaged to increase the installed capacity by 275 mW, but the actual achievements fell short of the proposed targets due to the delay in commissioning of various units of Bhakra Right Bank, Ranapratap Sagar and Satpura Projects. However, the installed generating capacity increased by 95.69 mW from 134.568 mW at the end of Second Plan to 230.258 mW at the end of Third Five Year Plan.

The Fourth Five Year Plan scheduled to start from 1966-67 was postponed for three years due to lack of financial resources. During these three years all the five units (each of 120 mW) at Bhakra Right Bank Power Project, first three units (each of 43 mW) at Rana Pratap Sagar Project and the first four units (each of 62.5 mW) at Satpura Thermal Station were commissioned. Thus the installed capacity of Rajasthan increased to 472.83 mW by the end of 1968-69, the details of which are given in Table 3A.2. An ambitious power plan was prepared for the Fourth Five Year Plan which added 108 mW generating installed capacity raising it to 580.83 mW at the end of the Fourth Plan. The installed capacity continued to increase up to the capacity of 1796.81 mW was achieved ending March 1986.

With the growth in generation capacity, it is imperative to develop a system for power transmission from the generation sources to load centres. Starting with zero level in 1949, a substantial transmission system has been developed in the State during past forty years. Table 3A.3 narrates the story of evolution and development of transmission lines in the State.

TABLE 3A.3: Growth of Transmission System

		Achievement by March 31				
Transmission	Unit	1949	1961	1969	1979	1985
220 kV Lines	km	—	—	115	1250	2666
220 kV S/s	mVA	—	—	35	670	1905
132 kV Lines	km	—	321	1753	3967	5950
132 kV S/s	mVA	—	6	202	1332	2225
66 kV Lines	km	—	232	412	415	386
66 kV S/s	mVA	—	8	45	57	57

400 kV transmission system is also being introduced in Rajasthan. National Thermal Power Corporation (NTPC) has constructed a 400 kV line from Kanpur to Jaipur for supply of power from Singrauli Thermal Power Station. The 400 kV Grid Sub-Station installed by Rajasthan State Electricity Board was commissioned in December 1986. There was no extra high voltage transmission (EHT) system at the time of formation of the State of Rajasthan. Sub-transmission system comprised of 136 km of 33 kV and 192 km 11 kV lines, was the only transmission-network to supply the then installed capacity of 30.27 mW. Today, the State has well-developed (100354 km) transmission and wide-spread (106946 km) distribution-network to supply the power, generated by installed capacity of the order of 1797 mW. But it still a matter of further investigation that how much of power-requirements for socio-economic activities of the State is being fulfilled by the existing power-network.

Certain geopolitical and techno-economical factors influence the installation, generation and supply of power. Prestigious units of Rajasthan Atomic Power Project of an installed capacity of 440 mW, have never been able to work in full swing due to technological hindrances. Generation capacities of hydel power projects are controlled by erratic monsoon. Paying capacity of consumers and purchasing power of the Board inhibit them from having adequate quantum of power due to financial shortfall. Politically motivated unjust decisions produce disparities in resource allocation and generate malpractice in plan implementation.

Schemes at Work

In Rajasthan effective steps to meet the projected scarcity of electricity have been initiated by the Government but there is no doubt the State would face a heavy deficit at the end of the Seventh Plan. Besides financial constraints there is a ticklish problem of locating new sources of energy. Being situated far from water power potential areas, Rajasthan is dependent for its power needs on hydel sources and the projects executed in this respect desire to establish inter-State understanding. That is why during 1985-86, out of the total installed capacity of 1797 mW nearly 59 per cent share accounted for inter-State power projects and remaining 41 per cent from local power plants and.

RAPP. More possibilities of establishing State-owned power projects are being explored to meet the power shortage. Some of the under-construction power generating schemes are mentioned here:

(1) *Mahi-Bajaj Sagar Project* – It is a joint venture of the State of Rajasthan and Gujarat. In the First State 1×25 mW set is being installed at Saddle Dam No. 5 of Mahi reservoir situated near Banswara-Ratlam road, 10 km away from Banswara. In addition a set of 45 mW capacity, has been proposed to be installed in the Second Stage Power Station. It will cost Rs. 82 crores.

(2) *Kota Thermal Project* – This project in its First Stage had two units of 110 mW each and in the Second Stage two more units of capacity of 220 mW have been proposed to be installed at the cost of Rs. 452 crores.

(3) *Anoopgarh Mini Hydel Scheme* – The scheme proposed on the Anoopgarh Branch of Indira Gandhi Canal in Sriganganagar district will utilize the force of lifted water-falls at R.D.-15 and RD-60 consisting of two power houses with an installed capacity of 2(3×1.5) mW. A sum of Rs. 650.60 lac is estimated for this scheme. It will generate 788 lakh units of power per year after completion of the scheme.

(4) *Suratgarh Mini Hydel Power Project*: This mini hydel scheme will consist of two units of installed capacity of 2 mW utilizing the force of four water falls near Lakhiwala on the Suratgarh Branch of Indira Canal. It will provide 219 lakh units of power per year to the State.

(5) *Mangrol Hydel Scheme*: A 6 mW capacity (3×2 mW) Power station proposed to be installed near Mangrol at Right Main Canal of Chambal Project, will utilize the force of five water-falls through a loop-canal. It will cost Rs. 611.15 lakh and produce 526 lakh units of power per year.

(6) *Charanwala Mini Hydel Scheme*: With an estimated cost of Rs. 286 lakh a 2 mW generating set is proposed to be installed on the Charanwala Branch of Indira Canal. This power station will utilize the hydel force of two water-falls of Charanwala Branch Canal.

(7) *Pugal Hydel Power Scheme*: Two power stations of 1500 kW and 650 kW capacity, are proposed to be installed at Pugal Branch of

Indira Canal at an estimated cost of Rs. 438.12 lakh. These stations will generate 188 lakh units of additional power to the State.

(8) *Jakham Mini Hydel Power Project*: This scheme had been proposed envisaging generation of 9 mW capacity (2×4.5 mW) near village Dhariawad in Chittorgarh district. An Irrigation dam is under-construction by the Department of irrigation on River Jakham. The power station will utilize the hydel force of water-falls laying between the dam and Nagalia Pic-up. An additional quantum of power of the order or 363.63 lakh units will be available after completion of the scheme costing Rs. 1292.94 lakh.

(9) *Jaisalmer (Ramgarh) Gas-Thermal Scheme*: A scheme has been prepared by the Government to install a 3 mW gas-thermal power station at Ramgarh town in Jaisalmer district utilizing the natural gas found in Manohar Tiba. It will cost Rs. 394 lakh.

(10) *Palana Lignite Thermal Power Station*: The Palana Project had been proposed to install a thermal power station consisting of two units of 60 mW capacity each. The 2×60 mW Power House will generate electricity at 60 per cent load factor for 25 years utilizing the lignite of of Palana coal field near Bikaner. The revised estimated cost of the plant is Rs. 297 crores including Rs. 117 crores for lignite-mining and Rs. 180 crores for construction and installation of power house.

In addition, several schemes are under consideration of the State Government, and some of them have finalised and sent to the Planning Commission for financial consideration. These schemes are shown in Table 3A.4. Two Gas Thermal Power Stations at Sawai Madhopur and Banswara, based on Bombay High Gas, each with a planned capacity of 400 mW at a consolidated cost of Rs. 251 crores were proposed to CEA. However, as a policy the Government of India has decided to take up these projects in the central sector. The Government has taken decision to set up a 500 mW station of this type at Anta (Kota) in Seventh Five Year Plan, the benefits of which are likely to accrue early in the Eighth Five Year Plan.

TABLE 3A.4: Schemes under Consideration of Planning Commission

	Scheme	Situation	Capacity in kW	Cost in lakh Rs.
1	Mahi Right-Main Canal Mini-Hydel I	Near Ghatol	2X400	132.56
2.	Itawa Mini-Hydel Right Main Chambal	Near Ganeshganj on Itawa Branch Canal	1X500	109.57
3.	Virsalpur Hydel Scheme on Indira Canal	On Virsalpur Branch Canal RDG 120 & RD 130	1X535 1X165 1X220	281.00
4.	Mahi-Right-Main-Canal Mini Hydel II	Near Vill. Bhuasa in Banswara on RD 55331	1X165	34.04
5.	Nachana Mini Hydel Indira Main Canal	Near Bikampur Village in Jaisalmer Distt. on Nachana-distributary	1X175	40.65
6.	Jaluwala Mini Hydel Jaluwala distributory of Indira Canal	Near Village Charanwala in Jaisalmer district	1X90	26.31
7.	Khara Mini Hydel	Near Vill. Bajju in Bikaner on Khara distributing of Indira Canal	1X125	40.99
8.	Phulasar Mini Hydel	On Phulasar distributory of Indira Canal in Bikaner distt.	1X280	78.57
Total kW capacity and cost of installation			3055	743.69

Source: Annual Report 1985-86, RSEB pp 12-13.

3B. Growth of Power Consumption in Rajasthan

Rajasthan has made gigantic strides in the field of power generation and supply during the past fifteen years although it is still feeling the pinch of power shortage. The power scenario is, however, fast changing despite the bad historic legacy and absence of perennial hydel source and fossil fuels in the State. The progress made by the State in the field of electricity utilization is significant keeping in view that the State, when formed in 1949, had only 13.27 mW of power. Figure 3B.1 shows the areal growth pattern of power consumption at district level for 15 years, exhibiting highly differentiated form of power distribution.

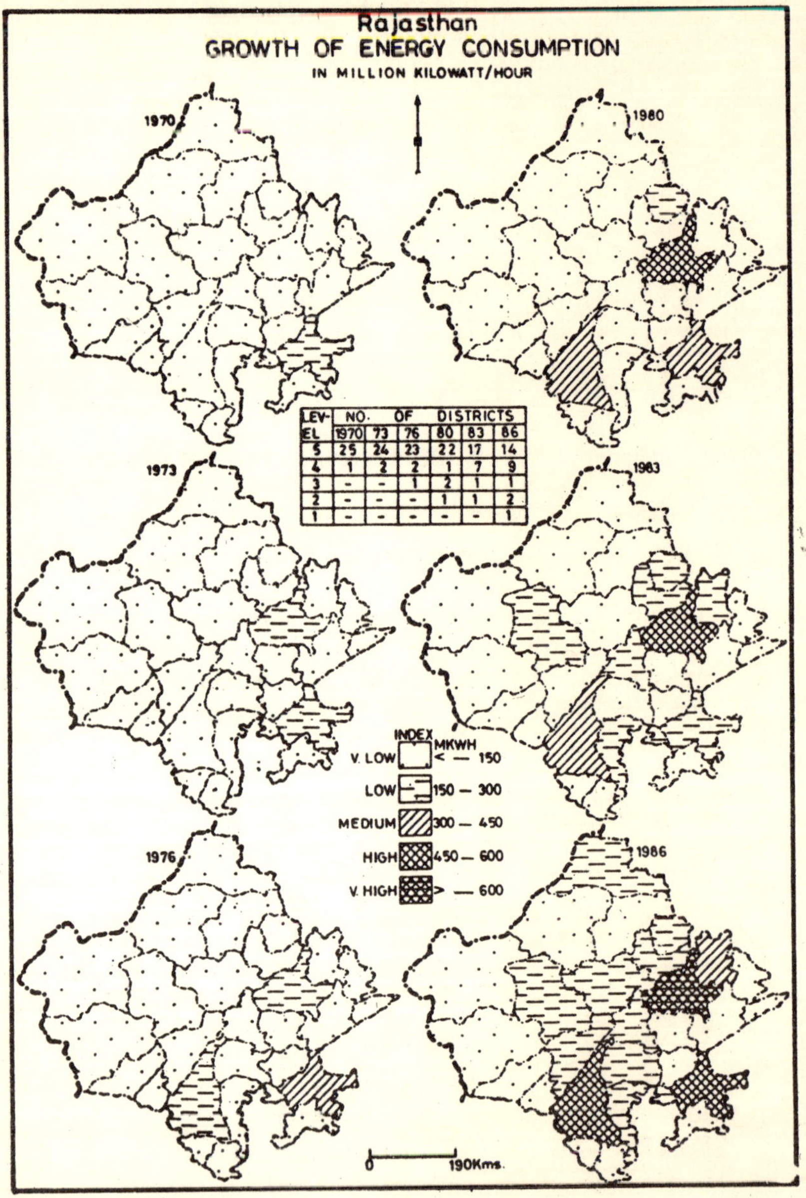

LEVEL	NO. OF DISTRICTS					
	1970	73	76	80	83	86
5	25	24	23	22	17	14
4	1	2	2	1	7	9
3	-	-	1	2	1	1
2	-	-	-	1	1	2
1	-	-	-	-	-	1

FIG. 3B.1

To compute the growth rate of power consumption in Rajasthan on the basis of past trend of power utilization in the State, 15 years data of sectoral power consumption have been taken into consideration. Sector-wise growth rate of power utilization has been computed applying the following formula (Semi-Logarithmic):

$$b = \frac{\Sigma t \log Y}{\Sigma t^2} \qquad (3.1)$$

where t = Points of time under consideration and
y = Power consumption of a particular sector

$$gr = (A1b - 1)\,100 \qquad (3.2)$$

where gr denotes the growth rate of power consumption of a particular sector

Al = Antilog of b

Growth rates of power consumption for seven sectors of economy have been calculated separately along with the growth rate of aggregate power consumption in Rajasthan. Details of the computation of sectoral growth rates are given in Appendix. Aggregate growth rate has been computed in Table 3B.1.

TABLE 3B.1: Computation of Growth rate of Power Consumption in Rajasthan

Years	t	t^2	Y (mkW)	$\log Y$	$t \log Y$
1970-71	–7	49	958.924	2.9818	–20.8726
1971-72	–6	36	1104.456	3.0431	–18.2586
1972-73	–5	25	1261.581	3.1009	–15.5045
1973-74	–4	16	1331.460	3.1243	–12.4972
1974-75	–3	9	1564.410	3.1943	–9.5829
1975-76	–2	4	1822.656	3.2607	–6.5214
1976-77	–1	1	2107.396	3.3237	–3.3237
1977-78	0	0	2267.980	3.3556	0
1978-79	1	1	2724.821	3.4353	3.4353
1979-80	2	4	2968.995	3.4726	6.9452
1980-81	3	9	2928.961	3.4667	10.4001
1981-82	4	16	3131.401	3.4957	13.9829
1982-83	5	25	3268.789	3.5143	17.5719
1983-84	6	36	4148.710	3.6179	21.7074
1984-85	7	49	4386.555	3.6421	25.4948
Total		280		50.0290	12.9767

The semi-logarithmic computation provides the following equation:

$$
\begin{aligned}
b &= 12.9767 \div 280 = 0.04634 \\
Gr &= (\text{ALb} - 1)\ 100 \\
&= (1.112616 - 1)\ 100 \\
&= .112616 \times 100 \\
&= 11.26\ \%
\end{aligned}
$$

On the basis of experience of last fifteen years, the growth rate of electricity consumption in Rajasthan, is computed 11.26 per cent. The same has been calculated for individual sectors applying the above mentioned formula.

Table 3B.2 depicts the sector-wise growth of power consumption in Rajasthan using 15 years data from 1970-71 to 1984-85. The agricultural sector experienced (19.3%) maximum rate of growth of power utilization followed by domestic (14.15%), commercial (11.16%), water supply (9.93%), Industrial (8.11%) and public lighting (7.79%). The agriculture sector exhibited 8.04 per cent higher consumption rate of growth than that of the gross-growth rate (11.26%) and domestic sector showed 2.89 per cent higher rate than the gross rate. Commercial sector equalled by the gross rate while rest of the sectors remained below the gross growth rate ranging between 1 per cent and 5 per cent. It is interesting to note that greater emphasis has been given on agriculture, where the bulk of State's population is engaged.

TABLE 3B.2: Sectoral Growth Rates of Power-Consumption in Rajasthan

Sl. No.	Sector	Σt^2	$\Sigma t \log Y$	$\frac{\Sigma t \log Y}{t^2}$	(ALb-1)100	Growth rate per cent
1.	Agriculture	280	21.4601	.076643	(1.193007—1)100	19.30
2.	Domestic	280	16.1017	.057506	(1.141579—1)100	14.15
3.	Commercial	280	12.8731	.045975	(1.1116677—1)100	11.16
4.	Public water	280	11.5099	.041106	(1.0992471—1)100	9.93
5.	Public light	280	9.1299	.032607	(1.0779708—1)100	7.79
6.	Industrial	280	9.4927	.0333902	(1.081189—1)100	8.11
7.	Mix-load	280	7.2028	.025724	(1.061021—1)100	6.10
	Total	280	12.9767	.04634	(1.112602-1)100	11.26

Pattern of Power Demand in the Past

Table 3B.3 provides the proportion of electricity consumed by different categories of consumers in the State in various years from 1957-58. The table shows that the single major sector that consumes the bulk share of power in Rajasthan, as in other States, is industries sectors, constituted by small, medium and large scale industries. The share of these industries has been between 36 to 59 per cent in all the years from 1957-58 to 1985-86. The share of power under the industrial sector increased by 23 per cent from 1957-58 to 1977-78, and declined by 13 per cent afterwards. This decline in the share of industries sector in power consumption was accompanied by a significant increase in the share of agricultural sector. This sector, as seen from the table, accounted for only 4.21 per cent in 1957-58. However, this has gradually increased to 32.77 per cent in 1981-82 and further decline to 30.23 per cent in 1985-86. The increasing share of power in the agricultural sector without an increase in State's power generation capacity, created an imbalance between demand and supply. Considering this imbalance, authorities decided to go slow in agriculture load development from 1982 onwards. This is reflected by a drop in the share of this sector after 1981-82. The domestic sector first exhibited declining trend in the share of power consumption falling down from 16.81 per cent in 1957-58 to 6.88 per cent in 1979-80. Since then the sector showed an increase in the share rising to 9.63 per cent in 1985-86. Commercial sector followed the same trend that of the domestic sector.

TABLE 3B.3: Pattern of Power Demand in Rajasthan (Past Trend)

(Percentage of Total Consumption)

Sector	1957-58	1967-68	1977-78	1978-80	1981-82	1983-84	1985-86
Industrial	35.65	53.63	58.96	49.54	44.63	47.93	45.93
Agriculture	4.21	9.04	19.77	30.86	32.77	31.38	30.23
Domestic	16.81	9.14	6.98	6.88	8.26	8.20	9.63
Commercial	16.21	9.21	5.23	4.72	5.17	4.73	5.41
Water supply	21.57	7.84	5.01	4.49	5.04	4.36	5.01
Mix load	—	9.32	3.25	2.83	3.55	2.82	3.11
Street light	5.55	1.80	0.80	0.68	0.58	0.58	0.68
mkWh	50.959	407.599	2267.980	2968.995	3131.401	4148.710	4808.0

Thus, the two most noteworthy and striking features in the pattern of power demand in the past, are the decline in the share of industrial sector and the increase in the share of agricultural sector. Probably this kind of structural change in the power consumption pattern is peculiar to Rajasthan. In contrast to this, in Madhya Pradesh the proportion of electricity used by industrial sector increased from 59.4 per cent in 1950 to 81 per cent in 1976. This peculiar pattern in Rajasthan is perhaps indicative of the slow progress in the industrial sector. It was agricultural sector which took more advantage of rural electrification in the State.

Power Projection for Rajasthan

Sector-wise power projection up to AD 2000 has been computed in Table 3B.4 so as to find out the pattern of future power demand in Rajasthan, calculated in Table 3B.5. To compute the power projections, Semi-Logarithmic exponential forms *$\text{Log } Y = a+bt$ have been taken into consideration. Where Y is demand and t is point of time. Values are estimated statistically using time series data relating to the period from 1970-71 to 1984-85. The estimated equations for different categories of consumers of power in Rajasthan, are given below:

(i) Agricultural Consumers
$\text{Log } Y = 2.7014 + 0.076643 \times t$

(ii) Industrial Consumers
$\text{Log } Y = 3.06009 + 0.0339041 \times t$

(iii) Domestic Consumers
$\text{Log } Y = 2.1895 + 0.0575061 \times t$

(iv) Commercial consumers
$\text{Log } Y = 2.0459 + 0.0459753 \times t$

(v) Water Supply Consumers
$\text{Log } Y = 2.0393 + 0.0411067 \times t$

(vi) Mix Load Consumers
$\text{Log } Y = 1.9024 + 0.0257244 \times t$

(vii) Street Lighting Consumers
$\text{Log } Y = 1.2088 + 0.032607 \times t$

---

* Pillai P.P. (1984) "Regional Power Scenario in 2001 AD: Case of Kerala" in *Indian Journal of Regional Science*, Vol. XVI, No. 1 pp 46-53.

(viii) Aggregate in Rajasthan

$$\text{Log } Y = 3.3353 + 0.0463442 \times t$$

TABLE 3B.4: Power Demand Projection for Rajasthan in mkWH

Sector	1985-86 $t = 8$	1989-90 $t = 12$	1994-95 $t = 17$	1999-2000 $t = 22$	Y = a+bt
Agriculture	1841.071	3160.9543	5984.505	10998.029	(3.061+.044559)t
Industrial	2144.484	2930.483	4329.719	6397.056	(3.06009+.0339041)t
Domestic	446.219	757.832	1469.277	2848.618	(2.1895+0.0575061)t
Commercial	259.240	395.916	672.171	1141.186	(2.0459+0.0459753)t
Water supply	233.428	340.489	546.309	876.545	(2.0393+0.0411067)t
Mix load	128.291	162.589	218.633	293.993	(1.9024+0.0257244)t
Street light	29.489	39.818	57.959	84.363	(1.2088+0.032607)t
Rajasthan	5082.222	7788.080	13278.573	22639.790	(3.335+0.0463442)t

On the basis of these estimated exponential trends in the consumption of electricity by various categories of consumers the likely demand in future years up to AD 2000, has been computed in Table 3B.4. The table depicts that by the turn of the century, all the sectors of economy in Rajasthan will have to have as much quantum of power as 22639.79 million kilowatt hour which is 4.7 times higher than that of the actual power consumption during 1985-86. Authorities have to decide whether they will be able to make a fivefold increase in the present capacity of power-generation or they will allow to widen the gulf between demand and supply.

TABLE 3B.5: Pattern of Power Demand in Rajasthan (Future Trend)

(Percentage of total Consumption)

Sector	1985-86	1989-90	1994-95	1999-2000
Agriculture	36.23	40.59	45.07	48.58
Industries	42.20	37.63	32.61	28.26
Domestic	8.78	9.73	11.06	12.58
Commercial	5.10	5.08	5.06	5.04
Water Supply	4.59	4.37	4.11	3.87
Mix Load	2.52	2.09	1.65	1.30
Street Light	0.58	0.51	0.44	0.37
mkWh	5082.222	7788.080	13278.573	22639.79

Estimated Pattern of Power Demand in Future

The above projections (Table 3B.5) indicate a change in the pattern of category-wise demand for electricity in the State in future. By the close of the present century, the demand for electricity by the agriculture sector would be 48.58 per cent of the total demand in the economy of the State, equal to the demand once attained by the industrial sector during 1979-80. In contrast to agricultural demand of power, the proportion of electricity demand by industrial sector is estimated only 28.26 per cent of the total power demand of the State, sharing nearly 3 per cent less than that of the share (30.86%) once attained by agriculture during 1979-80. The domestic sector would form about 12.6 per cent of the aggregate demand in AD 2000, followed by commercial (5%), water supply (3.87%), mix load (1.3%) and street lighting (0.37%) consumers. The most striking feature of the future pattern of power demand described in Table 3B.5, is that all the consumers of power in Rajasthan, would tend to decrease their share in total power demand except the domestic and agriculture consumers. It is again shocking to note that the power supply (4808.011 mkWh) remained below the projected quantum of power (5082.222) by 274.211 mkWh (or 5.7%) for the year 1985-86. The year of 1985-86 has been selected as a common point of time as an ending year of the Past Demand Trend (Table 3B.3) and the starting year of Future Demand Trend (Table 3B.5) so as to assess the difference between power supply and power demand projection. The difference was assessed as much as (–) 5.7 per cent for the same year in terms of aggregate power demand in the State. Agricultural consumers were provided with 30.23 per cent (1453.643 mkWh) of total power during 1985-86 as against 36.23 per cent (1841.071 mkWh) projected for the same year, while the industrial sector was given 45.93 per cent (2208.188 mkW) in comparison to estimated demand of 42.4 per cent (2144.484 mkWh) of the aggregate power. The State Electricity Board had decided to go slow in agriculture load development from 1982 on wards which is reflected by decreasing trend in percentage of total power distribution for agriculture. The supply of power requires to be continuously augmented to meet the ever-increasing demand of production not only in agriculture but in all sectors of economy. Therefore authorities should mobilise all its resources to produce more and more power to fasten the rate of economic growth in the State.

Gulf Between Demand and Supply of Power

The two phenomena – demand and supply – in power sector of Rajasthan, were balanced till the seventies. The developing load of power in the late seventies and early eighties, without a proportionate increase in generation capacity, created an imbalance between demand and supply. This imbalance has been explained in Table 3B.6 and Fig. 3B.2. The demand together with availability and supply of power have been taken into account so as to reckon the shortfall and losses of power in the State. The table shows that 2929 mkWh were supplied to the consumers as against a demand of 4889 mkWh during 1980-81, thus creating a shortfall of 40.1 per cent. The shortfall of power rose near to 52 per cent during 1982-83, and since then it is going on a declining trend. It is estimated that by the turn of the century there would be 40.1 per cent (15158 mkWh) shortfall between demand (37798 mkWh) and supply (22640 mkWh). Losses of power supply would tend to vary between 30 per cent and 13 per cent during 1980-81 to 1999-2000 AD. The emergence of high voltage and extra high voltage transmission lines have helped to reduce the percentage of losses of power while transmitting and distributing it among the consumers situated far away from the generation plants. However it is clear from the table that even if authorities raise periodically the quantum of power-supply, the State may be ending up with a power deficit to the order of 9487 mkWh by 1995 and 15158 mkWh by 2000 AD. The only solution would be to raise the generation capacity of existing power plants and install new ones so as to bridge the gulf between demand and supply of electricity in Rajasthan.

New trends in agricultural growth and massive efforts on industrial development have tremendously multiplied the State's requirement for more power. Sector-wise computation of the difference between demand and supply (Table 3B.7) for the year 1985-86, exhibits 46.6 per cent shortfall for commercial consumers followed by industrial (39.3%), agriculture (22.67%), and water supply sector (5.12%). Mix load, street lighting and domestic consumers exhibited surplus power consumption as against their estimated demand. Industries in Rajasthan, were provided with 2208 mkWh of power as against the demand of 3638 mkWh, thus created a deficit of 1430 mkWh for the sector. Similarly, the agricultural sector consumed 1453 mkWh as against 1879 mkWh of requirement. Consuming 76 per cent power of the State, the industrial and agricultural sector carried 94 per cent deficit during 1985-86. Power shortage seemed to have added a new dimension to the ideological differences over granting priorities to industry and agriculture. Power supplies were being stopped specifically for providing interim relief either to industry or to agriculture at the cost of the other.

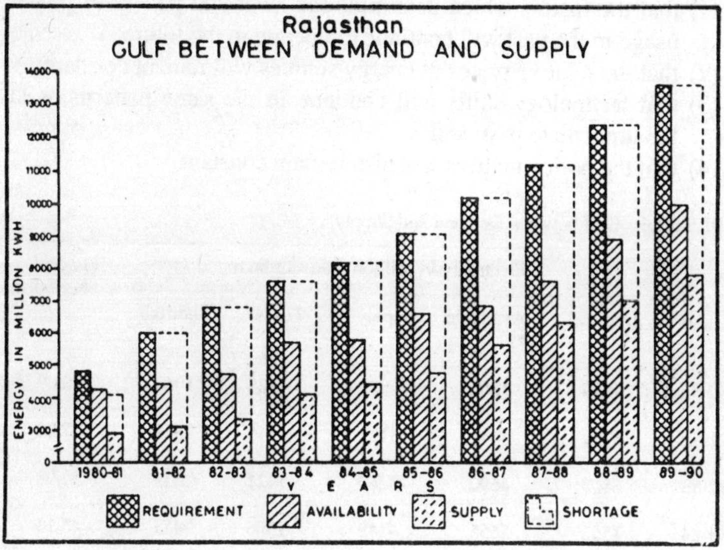

FIG. 3B.2

Bias in the Forecasting Power Demand

There is a basic problem with the forecasting procedure using the regression equation. The equation uses recent historical power consumption data as the basis for projecting future power consumption. The problem with this approach is that if the power supply were inadequate during the recent past, this same inadequacy will be projected into the future periods. Hence, the use of this technique for predicting future power consumption demand amounts to planning for future shortage if shortage existed in the past. Every technique based on past period data produces the same result. The existence of power outages and power shortages during the base period means that consumption would have been higher with existing demand had the power been available. Power projections depend upon certain assumptions:

(1) that the factors which determine the level and pattern of power usage in the past will continue to operate in the future;
(2) that the relative prices of energy sources will remain constant;
(3) that technology shifts will continue in the same patterns as in the immediate past; and
(4) that the policy matters will also remain constant.

TABLE 3B.6: Gulf between Demand and Supply

Year	Electricity in Million Kilowatt hour					Per cent Shortfall
	Demand *2	Available *3	Supply *1	Losses	Shortfall	
1980-81	4889	4263	2929	1334	1960	40.09
1981-82	5999	4446	3131	1315	2868	47.80
1982-83	6808	4690	3269	1421	3539	51.98
1983-84	7562	5655	4149	1506	3413	45.13
1984-85	8197	5821	4387	1434	3810	46.48
1985-86	9133	6563	4808	1755	4325	47.35
1986-87	10164	6780	5654	1126	4510	44.37
1987-88	11245	7589	6291	1298	4954	44.06
1988-89	12391	8916	6999	1917	5392	43.52
1989-90	13613	9943	7788	2155	5825	42.79
1994-95	22766	15706	13279	2427	9487	41.67
1999-2000	37798	25653	22640	3013	15158	40.10

* 1. Estimated $\text{Log } Y = 3.3353 + 0.0463442 \times t$
* 2. Estimated $\text{Log } Y = 3.9609744 + 0.0440355 \times t$
* 3. Estimated $\text{Log } Y = 3.8125307 + 0.0426153 \times t$

TABLE 3B.7: Sectorwise Power Shortage, 1985-86

Sector	Demand mkW	Supply mkW	Shortfall Surplus	% Shortfall Surplus
Industries	3638	2208	-1430	-39.31
Agriculture	1879	1453	-426	-22.67
Domestic	461	463	(+) 2	(+) 0.43
Commercial	487	260	-227	-46.61
Water Supply	254	241	-13	-5.12
Mix Load	30	150	(+) 120	(+) 400.00
Street Light	32	33	(+) 1	(+) 3.12
Total	6781	4808	-1973	-29.09
T & D Loss	2352	1439	-913	-38.82
Total	9133	6247	-2886	-31.60

4

ENERGY CONSUMPTION PATTERN IN RAJASTHAN

TODAY, WE have entered in an era of mechanical civilisation, which is a high energy civilisation. Without having adequate supply of power, man would have little use of machines, and, in fact, could not build them. We are all familiar with the fact that the low energy consuming society is concerned with low energy technique. Similarly, the high energy consuming society is associated with its highly evolved technique. The history of energy consumption involves gigantic developments in energy fuel used and these have had an immense economic and social impact on life. These developments include such changes as a shift of energy fuel, from wood to coal in the 19th century, an enormous growth of liquid fuels after the two World Wars, and more tremendously the growth of electrification throughout the 20th century. Inanimate energy played a minor role in the world energy consumption around the year 1800, and even until 1850 the inanimate energy was still less important than the animate. In the late 19th century and the beginning of the 20th century the entire development was necessarily carried on a single base-coal; subsequently oil and electricity took over along with natural gas at a later stage.

In the preceding chapter an attempt has been made to analyze energy network pattern of Rajasthan evaluating high and low voltage transmission and distribution lines the means of power supply. The present section of the study, deals with the consumption pattern of power supplied to different socio-economic sectors. Six such sectors have been taken into consideration that play an important part in the utilization of power (Appendix Table 4.1) : (a) domestic, (b) commercial, (c) industrial, (d) agricultural, (e) water supply, (f) public illumination. Growth trend of consumers, also has been taken into account for each one of the sectors depending on the data available. Simultaneously, this chapter is devoted to examine districtwise sectoral power use pattern.

4A. Domestic Power Consumption Pattern

Almost all types of fuels are being utilized today in Rajasthan for domestic purposes. Dung-cakes, firewood, agricultural wastes and *gobar*-gas are important fuels used in rural sectors, whereas, kerosene, soft-coke, charcoal, lignite, towngas, liquified petroleum gas and electricity are significant in urban sector. Animal dung, firewood and vegetable wastes, the so-called non-commercial fuels, predominantly used in rural houses, account for the bulk of energy consumption in the domestic sector. This sector is a major energy consumer in Rajasthan since using both commercial and non-commercial fuels. The study is restricted to electricity consumption due to the non-availability of data as well as other factors that limit the work.

An Observation of Some Survey Reports

The energy requirement for cooking and lighting represents substantial portion of the energy needs and this is likely to remain so during this century. Obviously, the energy consumption in other sectors of economy is rapidly increasing, the ever growing population will certainly increase the energy demand for domestic sector. It may be of interest to make a comparison of several survey reports produced on domestic energy requirement for India.

TABLE 4A.1: **Domestic Fuel use Comparison**

Energy Type	NCAER			ESIC		
	1960-61	1970-71	1975-76	1960-61	1970-71	1975-76
Coal & coke (m.t.)	3.166	8.158	12.508	2.8	9.2	20.0
Oil products (m.t.)	2.313	7.671	10.619	2.0	4.3	6.3
Electricity (Twh)	2.967	10.948	18.742	1.5	7.3	11.4
Fire wood (m.t.)	98.2	112.700	118.7	100.0	121.0	130.0
Dung Cake (m.t.)	52.3	59.6	63.7	54.0	60.0	63.0
Waste products (m.t.)	26.4	30.8	33.5	30.7	45.0	53.0

Source: Demand for energy in India by National Council of Applied Economic Research, New Delhi, 1966.

Table 4A.1 reveals that in NCAER survey the figures of coal, firewood and waste products are lower than that of figures given by Energy Survey of India Committee while those of electricity and oil products are higher. The increasing figure of coal, oil and electricity shows that the domestic consumers tend to utilize commercial fuels. Hence the study of electrical power consumption under domestic sector of Rajasthan is of significant consideration.

The 18th round survey of the National Sample Survey (1963-64) covered 21000 rural households and 4000 urban to estimate the domestic energy use.

TABLE 4A.2: NSS Estimates of Domestic Energy Use

(in kg Coal replacement/year)

Energy Type	Rural	Per cent	Urban	Per cent	Total
Coke	2.48	9.0	25.00	91.0	27.48
Coal	3.53	21.48	12.90	78.52	16.43
Fire wood	256.00	61.54	160.00	38.46	416.00
Electricity	0.36	3.85	9.00	96.15	9.36
Gas	–	0.00	0.79	100.00	0.79
Dung-cake	40.00	75.00	13.30	25.00	53.30
Charcoal	6.30	60.00	4.20	40.00	10.50
Kerosene	28.70	35.74	51.60	64.26	80.30
Other	9.35	73.62	3.35	26.38	12.70

The NSS estimates in Coal replacement terms are lower than that of the NCAER estimates. Rural estimates are higher than the urban sector because the rural people gather non-commercial fuels free of private costs.

The National Council of Applied Economic Research carried out two surveys in 1962 and 1977. Their estimates of three non-commercial fuels per capita consumption is given in Table 4A.3.

TABLE 4A.3: Per Capita Consumption in Kg/yr

Fuel Type/Year	1962	1977
Firewood	237	120
Vegetable Waste	28	95
Dung Cake	169	158

There is considerable uncertainty regarding domestic energy consumption in Rajasthan as well as in India. NCAER estimated the domestic consumption of 0.44 tonne of coal replacement per capita per annum or 1.2 kg daily per capita. The study conducted by Energy Survey of India Committee revealed the use of firewood in urban and rural areas is 0.41 kg and 0.5 kg/head/day respecting only about 10 per cent of this demand is fulfilled from forest in Rajasthan. Fuelwood demand has been projected in Table 4A.4.

TABLE 4A.4: Fuelwood Demand Projected for Rajasthan

Year	Population in lakhs	Fuelwood – Requirement in Lakh tonnes		
		Rural	Urban	Total
1981	342	45.72	5.49	51.21
1991	409	54.70	6.12	60.82
2001	490	65.33	7.86	73.19

Source: Rajasthan Forest Statistics, 1985.

TABLE 4A.5: Per Capita Domestic Energy in kWh

Sources	1960-61	1975-76	Variation
Commercial sources	12.6	56.7	44.1
Non Commercial sources	249.0	213.9	(–)35.1
Total	261.6	270.6	9.0

The per capital energy consumption shown by sources in the above table reveals about 22 per cent annual growth of commercial energy sources whereas a decline of 0.88 per cent is experienced in non-commercial sources. This is due to the higher efficiency of commercial fuels replacing the non-commercial ones. Thus the rate of growth in electricity is anticipated to be high.

Growth Trends of Household Power Connections

There were 33303 villages in the census 1971 which rose by 1665 to 34968 villages making an increase of about 5 per cent over the decade in 1981 Census. Adding 201 cities and towns there are 35169 localities providing residential facility for 343 lakh persons in Rajasthan. Number of households is increasing with the growing population. Thus the villages and towns are increasing in their number and extending their area. Residential land comprise a greater share of the developed land area. The number of domestic power consumers in Rajasthan, has showed faster rise than any other type of consumers. Also, out of the total consumers, the largest number of consumers belonged to the domestic category throughout the period under study. This sector was the second largest power consumer after industries till 1964-65. Since than it stands at third place after industrial and agricultural consumers though the number of consumers still higher than any other category. Table 4A.6 displays the growth trend and percentage of total consumers under the domestic consumers (Fig. 4.1).

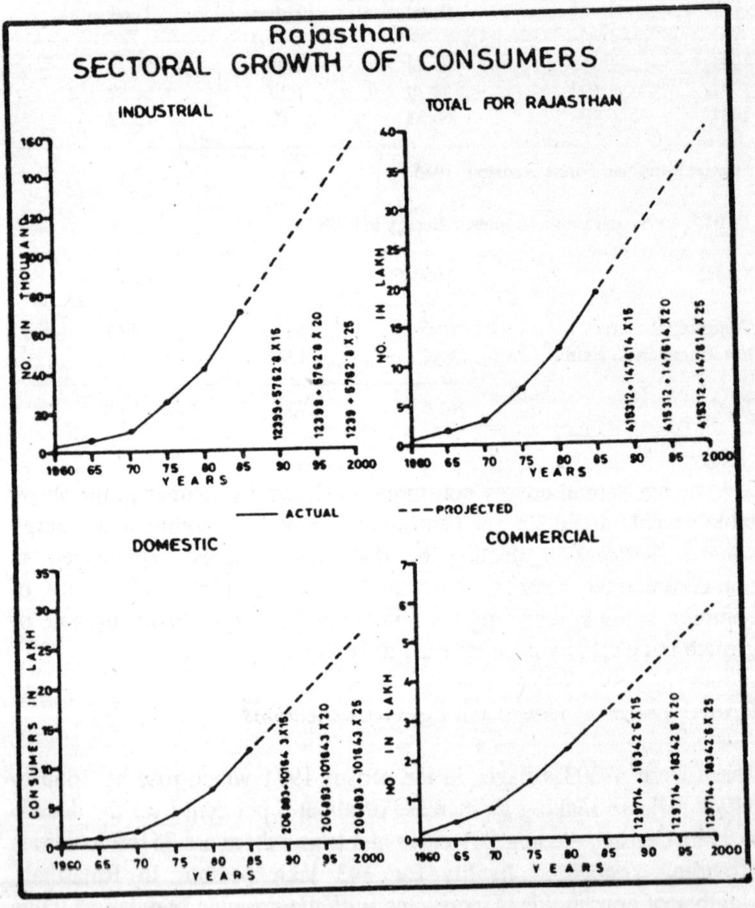

FIG. 4.1

TABLE 4A.6: Growth Trend of Household Connections

Year	Consumers	% of Total	Variation	% Variation
1959-60	51653	71.4	—	—
1964-65	124603	68.2	72950	141.23
1969-70	193930	64.96	69327	55.64
1974-75	425353	61.65	231423	119.33
1979-80	715108	62.0	289755	68.12
1984-85	1223323	64.7	508215	71.07
1989-90	1731538	65.85	508215	41.54
1994-95	2239753	66.51	508215	29.35
1999-2000	2747968	66.93	508215	22.69

TABLE 4A.7: Growth of Domestic Power Consumption (mkWh)

Year	Consumption	% of Total	Variation	% Variation
1959-60	11.679	21.5	—	—
1964-65	27.973	7.4	16.294	139.52
1969-70	52.833	6.7	24.860	88.87
1974-75	102.628	6.6	49.795	94.25
1979-80	204.330	6.9	101.702	99.10
1984-85	404.929	9.2	200.599	98.17
1989-90	606.000	10.5	201.071	49.66
1994-95	807.000	11.23	201.000	33.17
1999-2000	1008.000	11.74	201.000	24.90

Tables show that during the initial period of study 11.679 million kWh of power were consumed by 51653 households which rose to 404.929 mkWh being consumed by 12,23,323 households at the end of March 1985. At the end of March 1960, 226 kWh average per household power was available in Rajasthan which has increased to 331 kWh/household/year during 1984-85, and it is expected to rise to 385 kWh per household by this century. The percentage of domestic consumers (of the aggregate power consumers) declined from 71.4 per cent in 1960 to 61.65 per cent in 1975, which again rose to 64.7 per cent of the total in the year 1984-85. While the percentage of domestic power consumption varied between 6 per cent to 9 per cent throughout the study period except the initial year when it was 21.5 per cent of the total consumption. This was due to greater priority given to the sector and less attention towards the agricultural sector. The number of consumers and the consumption have been increasing since the very beginning but the highest growth was recorded in 1965, when the number of consumers increased by 141.2 per cent over the previous five years and the consumption increased by 139.5 per cent due to priorities given to domestic connections by the State Electricity Board.

District-wise Domestic Power Consumption Pattern

The large portion of the population of Rajasthan lives under unsatisfactory conditions relative to the living conditions elsewhere in India as well as in relation to the standards enjoyed by the other residents of the state. Relative distribution of power and other necessities of life over time and space are a useful means of focussing on the living conditions. The proportion of population living under sub-human conditions in absolute terms is also equally large. Different indicators of the levels of living not only present the macro-level dimensions of the process of development, but also micro-level ones. Per capita power generation and consumption, and per capita income are some of the macro-level indicators. Distribution of household power consumption, on the other hand, is a micro-level indicator, and this has been analysed here in terms of time and space. Districtwise household-power-consumption for the years 1979-80 and 1984-85, has been taken into consideration for this purpose. District wise percentage of total power utilisation under the domestic sector and the growth over five years period has been calculated which is given in Appendix Table 4A-8.

Appendix Table 4A.8 exhibits the district-wise variations in domestic power consumption for three points of time viz., 1979-80, 1984-85 and 1989-90. The table reveals the fact that nearly 66 per cent of State's total domestic power was consumed by seven districts, namely, Ajmer, Bikaner, Jaipur, Jodhpur, Kota, Sriganganagar and Udaipur. Three districts, namely, Alwar, Bharatpur and Sikar shared nearly 11 per cent of the State's total whereas remaining 23 per cent of State's total domestic power was distributed among rest of the sixteen districts. The analysis of spatial domestic power distribution shows a greater degree of diversity ranging from 0.2 per cent in Jaisalmer district to 25.5 per cent in Jaipur district during 1984-85, and the same result is estimated for 1989-90.

4B. Commercial Power Consumption Pattern

Commercial sector of power consumption is more significant in towns and cities rather than villages. The use of land for non-residential purposes, constitutes about 6.2 per cent of the total developed area of the Indian cities. The correlation of the percentage of the developed area with the population of cities is not very significant. The commercial use covers below five per cent of the total developed area in various cities. However, some cities like Jaipur (9.5%) have a higher percentage of business area. The acreage distribution in commercial areas with respect to the population size of the cities, most of the cities fall below 0.1 acre per hundred persons of the city population. The city falling above the limit 0.1 acre, are Jaipur (0.18), Kota (0.16) and Udaipur (0.12).[1] It shows that these three cities have maximum acreage per hundred persons for commercial use. The reason for this high percentage of commercial use is that these cities being big centres for trade, commerce and recreation, have more banks, cinemas, restaurants, hotels and other commercial buildings. The markets are highly illuminated by tube lights along the roads as well as inside the shops which requires a considerable quantum of power.

Growth Trend of Commercial Consumers in Rajasthan

The number of commercial consumers of power continued to increase with the result that the consumption of electricity rose by 216.83 million kWh from 10.23 mkWh in 1959-60 to 227.061 mkW during 1984-85 (Fig. 4.1)

TABLE 4B.1: Growth Trend of Commercial Power Connections

Year	Consumers	% of Total	Variation	% Variation
1959-60	16696	23.1	—	—
1964-65	47605	26.1	30909	185.13
1969-70	77678	26.02	30073	63.17
1974-75	149468	21.66	71790	92.42
1979-80	221427	19.2	71959	48.14
1984-85	313140	16.56	91713	41.42
1989-90	404853	15.4	91713	29.29
1994-95	496566	14.9	91713	22.65
1999-2000	588279	14.6	91713	18.47

Table 4B.1 depicts that 18.9 per cent of the total power consumption in Rajasthan was utilised by 23.1 per cent commercial consumers of the aggregate for the state during 1959-60. The percentage of users of power remained 26 per cent during 1960-70 increasing by three per cent over the previous period, while the consumption, in view of the percentage of the total, decreased by 12 per cent from 18.9 per cent in 1960 to 7.1 per cent in 1965 and 5.8 per cent in 1970 (Fig. 4.2). And this decrease of the percentage tend to continue in the coming years due to priorities given to other sectors by the Government, particularly, rural electrification and tubewells. In spite of decreasing percentage of total, the number of commercial consumers has been increasing, making a steady rise in power consumption. This tendency of a steady increase in number and units, with the decreasing percentage of total will continue till the end of this century as revealed by the application of straight line fitting for forecasting.

Consumption Trend

Table 4B.2 reveals that the highest growth in the commercial energy utilization took place during 1964-65. In this year an increase of 164.5 per cent (16.8 mkW) over the span of five years was recorded on an average 33 per cent annual rate of growth. In the later years the rate of consumption growth varied between 12-15 per cent per annum from 1970 to 1985. As per arithmetic rate of increase (87 mkW over five years), the percent variation growth is expected to decrease to 7 per cent, 5 per cent and 4 per cent during 1986-1990, 1991-95, and 1996-2000 respectively (Figs. 4.3 and 4.4).

TABLE 4B.2: Growth Trend of Commercial Power Consumption

Year	mkWh	% of Total	Variation	% Variation
1959-60	10.230	18.9	—	—
1964-65	27.059	7.1	16.829	164.51
1969-70	45.550	5.8	18.491	68.34
1974-75	80.274	5.1	34.724	74.51
1979-80	140.089	4.7	59.815	74.51
1984-85	227.061	5.2	86.972	62.08
1989-90	314.000	5.4	86.939	38.30
1994-95	401.000	5.4	87.000	27.70
1999-2000	488.000	5.7	87.000	21.69

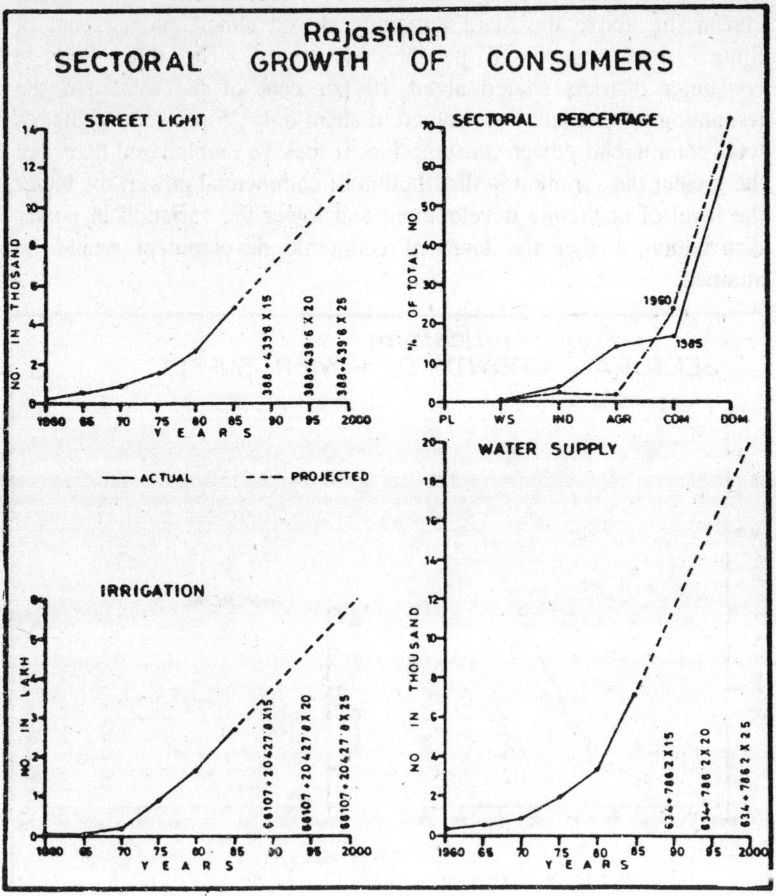

FIG. 4.2

District-wise Commercial Power Consumption Pattern

Appendix Table 4B.3 exhibits district-wise commercial power consumption pattern for three points of time viz., 1979-80, 1984-85 and 1989-90. The table reveals that Alwar, Bikaner and Pali districts were consuming the share of commercial power equal to State's average. Ajmer, Jaipur, Jodhpur, Kota, Sri Ganganagar and Udaipur district consumed above the State's average. While rest of the 17 districts remained below the State's average. The six districts consuming above the State's average shared almost 65 per cent of State's total commercial power consumption. The three average consumer districts shared about 10 per cent of the total and the remaining 17 districts were forced to share only 25 per cent of State's total commercial power consumption. It may be emphasized here that the greater the variation in distribution of commercial power, the lower the level of economic development and lower the variation in power distribution, higher the level of economic development would be attained.

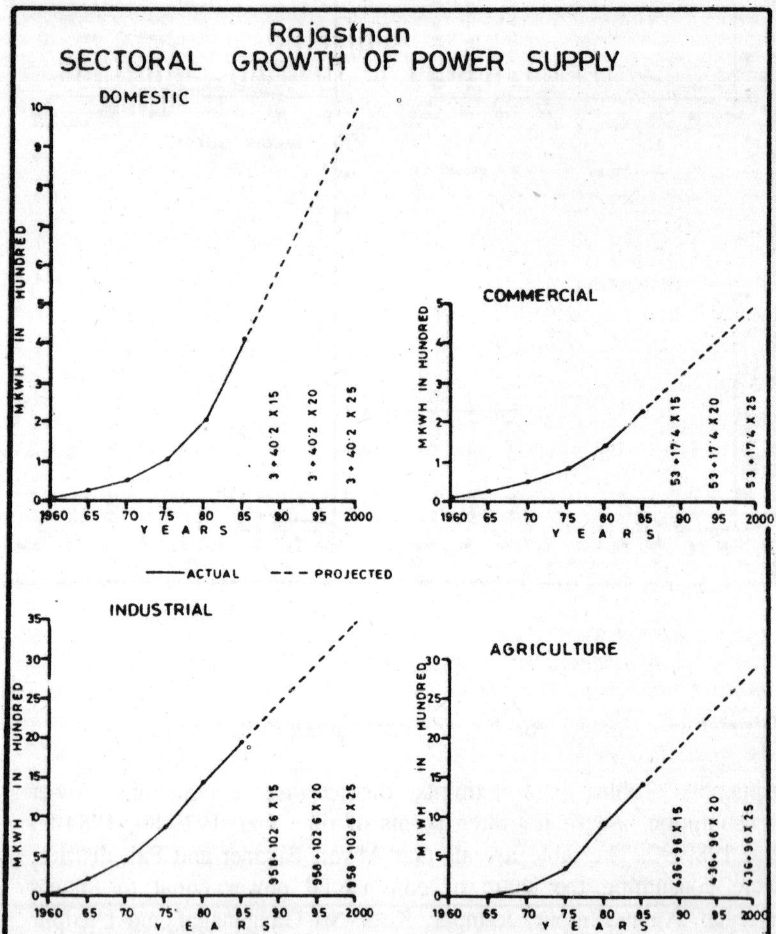

FIG. 4.3

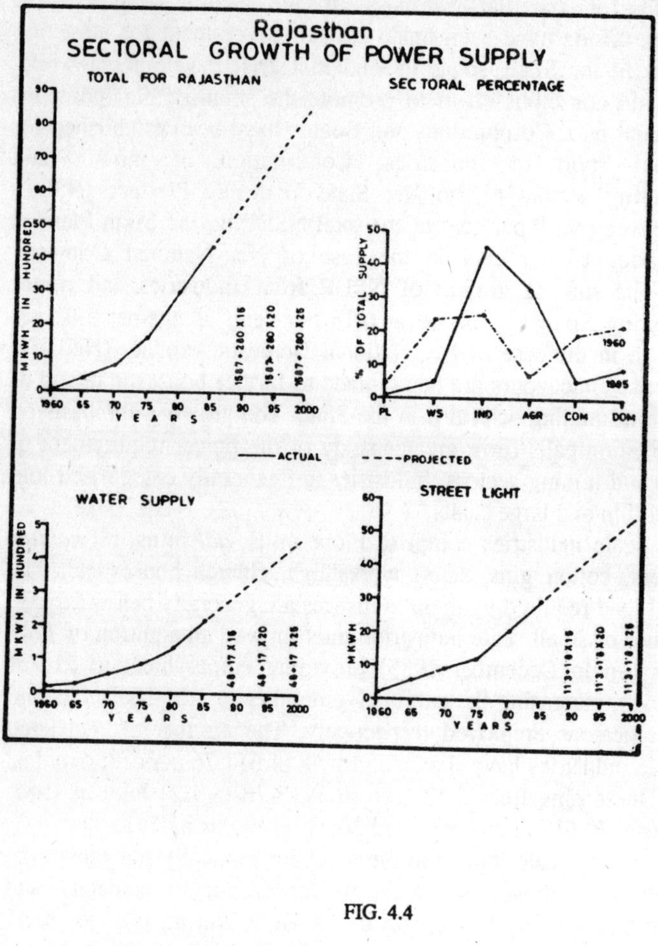

FIG. 4.4

4C. Industrial Power Consumption Pattern

The industrial development in India, has made rapid stride. This is evident from the remarkable widening of the industrial base and considerable diversification of its structure since independence.[2] Rajasthan is still an industrially backward State. The State had practically no industrial base and near total absence of infrastructure at the time of Independence. In addition to historical reasons and lack of infrastructure, the shortage of water and power is another factor responsible for the backwardness of the State. Despite these drawbacks, efforts have been made by the Government for attracting investment in the State, so as to lead industrial development while, there was no conscious effort to promote the small or big industries during feudal past. Corporations and Boards have been established for institutional sport to industries. Contribution of mining and manufacturing sectors to the Net State Domestic Product (NSDP) ranged between 9-10 per cent of the total NSDP during Sixth Plan, as against about 16 per cent in the case of Net National Domestic Product. The rate of growth of NSDP from Industries and mines sectors during Sixth Plan stood at 6.13 per cent, as against 5.62 per cent growth in the case of Net National Domestic Product (NNDP).[3] More intense endeavours are being made to further boost the tempo of industrial and mining activities in the State. The growing emphasis on industrialization calls for a greater study of the power requirement of industrial and mining sectors. Industries are generally categorised into small, medium and large scale.

Small scale industries comprise Flour mills, *dal* mills, oil *kohlus*, rice hullers, cotton gins, small workshops, cinema houses etc. The connected load required by these industries are generally below 20 kW. The number of small-scale industrial units showed an addition of 7745 industries (up to December 1985) providing employment to 21,922 lakh persons, increasing the cumulative number to 1.21 lakh units and 4.59 lakh persons employed respectively. The number of registered small scale industries have shown a growth of 611.76 per cent over last ten years increasing from 0.17 lakh in 1975-76 to 1.21 lakh in 1985. Out of these, 70,617 units consumed 264.4 mkW during 1985-86.

The medium scale industrial units cover practically the same type of activities as above, but with greater production capacity and connected load ranging between 25 to 100 BHP. During 1985-86, 4591 medium voltage industries consumed nearly 1·71 million kWh of power sharing only 7.74 per cent of State's total industrial power consumption. While the small-scale industries shared 11.96 per cent of the total industrial power consumption. Remaining 80.3 per cent power was utilised by large scale industrial units during 1985-86.

Large scale industries include large scale chemical, textile, metallurgic, electronic, cement and engineering industries. The number of factories registered with the Chief Inspector of Factories and Boilers have increased to 8233. The load demand for these units are assessed individually with detailed study of resources of raw materials and scope of development. The electro-chemical metallurgical industries constitute very important loads for the power system.

The State has witnessed considerable industrial growth during 1960-85 and this trend seems to continue in future also. There were only 2457 industrial consumers in 1959-60 which made 28.5 fold increase over 25 years. The highest growth of order of 161 per cent was exhibited in 1975 over the year 1970. By the turn of the century the industrial consumers are estimated to reach the number of 156,469 units. Consequently, the power requirement for industrial sector is likely to be doubled in the next 12 years (Figs. 4.1 and 4.3).

TABLE 4C.1: Growth Trend of Industrial Consumers

Year	Consumers	% of Total	Variation	% Variation
1959-60	2457	3.4	—	—
1964-65	5980	3.27	3523	143.39
1969-70	9674	3.24	3694	66.77
1974-75	25255	3.66	15581	161.06
1979-80	41213	3.57	15958	63.19
1984-85	70027	3.70	28814	69.91
1989-90	99841	3.80	29814	42.58
1994-95	127655	3.79	27814	27.86
1999-2000	156469	3.81	28814	22.57

TABLE 4C.2: Growth Trend of Industrial Power-Consumption (mkW)

Year	Consumption	% of Total	Variation	% Variation
1959-60	13.607	25.14	—	—
1964-65	234.312	61.7	220.705	1621.97
1969-70	467.248	59.5	232.936	99.41
1974-75	870.040	55.6	402.792	86.21
1979-80	1470.952	49.5	600.912	69.07
1984-85	1983.935	45.2	512.983	34.87
1989-90	2496.918	43.1	512.983	25.86
1994-95	3009.901	41.8	512.983	20.86
1999-2000	3522.884	41.0	512.983	17.04

The power consumption in industrial sector during 1959-60 was only 13.6 mkWh, 25 per cent of the State's total which has increased to 1984 mkWh during 1984-85, it is likely to become 3523 mkWh by the turn of the century leaving a big deficit ahead.

Consumption Pattern in Small, Medium and Large Scale Industries

Table 4C.3 displays consumption of power in small and medium, and large scale industrial units in Rajasthan for selected points of time. Clearly, the increasing energy consumption has been linked with industrial development. Despite the natural handicaps, as a result of policies and programmes initiated by the Government, the State has achieved considerable progress in industrial sector. To cite an example, the number of small and medium scale industrial consumers of power have gone up to 69.5 thousand in 1985 as against 2.4 thousand in 1960, increasing the power consumption up to 435 million units in 1985-86 as against only 12.4 million units in 1959-60. It is again interesting to note that the small and medium industrials utilized 91.6 per cent of total industrial power and 23 per cent of State's total power in 1959-60, which remained only 19.7 per cent and 9 per cent respectively in 1985-86. This shows the emphasis on large scale industrial development. Since 1965, the small and medium scale units shared 20.9 per cent of total industrial power consumption in the State, and rest of 79.1 per cent by large scale units. Moreover, nearly 50 per cent power of the State, has been consumed in industrial sector, of which 10 per cent in small and medium scale, and 40 per cent in large scale industries.

TALE 4C.3: Segregation of Power Consumption in Industrial Sector

Year	Small and Medium Scale			Large Scale Industries		
	Consumption in mkWh	% of industrial total	% of State's total	Consumption in mkWh	% of industrial total	% of State's total
1959-60	12.469	91.64	23.03	1.138	8.36	2.10
1964-65	44.621	19.04	11.74	189.691	80.96	49.92
1969-70	88.402	18.92	11.26	378.846	81.08	48.24
1974-75	167.807	19.29	10.73	702.233	80.71	44.89
1979-80	289.320	19.67	9.74	1181.632	80.33	39.80
1980-81	294.739	22.77	10.06	999.811	77.23	34.14
1981-82	331.372	23.73	10.58	1065.139	76.27	34.14
1982-83	351.318	27.01	10.75	949.285	72.99	29.04
1983-84	372.273	18.72	8.97	1616.282	81.28	38.96
1984-85	399.542	20.14	9.11	1584.393	79.86	36.12
1985-86	435.407	19.72	9.06	1772.781	80.28	36.87

Levels of Industrial Development in Rajasthan

Energy is an index of industrial development in itself. For an industrial advancement of the given region, it is essential to ensure adequate and sustained supply of power to industrial units. This exercise is attempted to compute the levels of industrial development in Rajasthan at district level on the basis of 1981 data. Five variables viz., (×1) number of factories, (×2) energy consumption, (×3) number of workers, (×4) input and (×5) output in million rupees have been taken into consideration. Values of these variables have been calculated into standardised value given in Appendix Table 4C.4 using the formula:

$$SV = \frac{X - \overline{X}}{SD}$$

Where $\overline{X}$ is the actual value of a variable, X is the mean value of the variable for all the districts of the State and *SD* is the standard deviation of the variable for the State.

A composite index is reckoned through the standardised values so as to assess the levels of industrial development of the State. All the districts have been grouped into five major categories in such a way that the districts having their index below the zero are termed as low and very low level of development, while those where the index lies between 0 to .5 are termed as medium level developed districts and finally the districts falling between 0.5 and 1 are termed high level whereas above 1 are termed as very high level of development. Table 4C.5 displays the levels of industrial development which again illustrated in Fig. 4C.5.

Table 4C.5 shows that nine districts were classified in very low and nine in the low level of development while three districts in medium range and only five districts were grouped in high and very high level of industrial development in Rajasthan. Thus, 21 districts out of 26 districts[4] are backward in view of industrial development in the State. According to the computation of appendix Table 4C.4, Jaipur, Kota and Udaipur districts have attained very High level of industrial development, Ajmer and Sri Ganganagar were categorised highly developed while Bhilwara, Jodhpur and Pali districts were grouped in medium level of development, and rest of the districts were still underdeveloped.

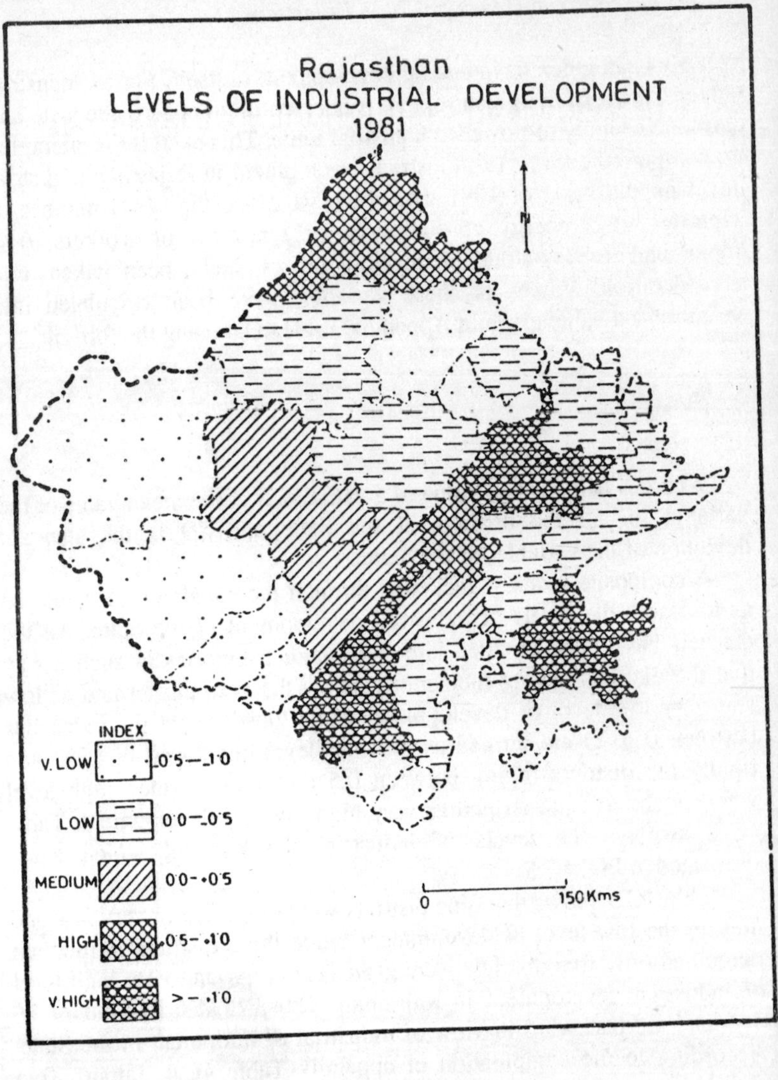

FIG. 4C.5

4D. Agricultural Power Consumption Pattern

Agriculture holds the key to the economy of the State, and nowhere in the country is the adage more true that agriculture is a gamble with monsoon, that in case of Rajasthan. As a result of erratic and insufficient rainfall, the State is witnessing unprecedented drought. The intensity of the gloomy situation can be measured by the fact that the production of foodgrains is expected to fall to around 63.37 lakh tonnes, as against a target of 95.70 lakh tonnes, while the level attained during even 1984-85 was 78.66 lakh tonnes.[5] The State has experienced great hardships due to weak and erratic monsoons since last seven years. In the background of absence of perennial rivers, vagaries and uncertainties of weather, means of irrigation are the life-line for the rural agro-based economy of Rajasthan. The vast stretches of land can be brought under plough to maximum possible extent only by extending the irrigation facilities. Wells and tubewells are the only hope to meliorate the situation as they constitute 55 to 63 per cent of the net irrigated area of the State (Table 4D.1).

Keeping in view the importance of wells in terms of percentage of net irrigated area, the State Government has put special emphasis on electrification of wells. Substantial progress has been made in this direction. There were only four thousand electrified wells in 1965 which rose to 282 thousand at the end of March 1986 (Fig. 4D.1). In spite of sustained efforts in agriculture pumpsets energisation, the area irrigated by tubewells is consistently on decline, which is shown in Table 4D.2.

TABLE 4C.5: Levels of Industrial Development in Rajasthan based on composite index computed in Appendix Table No. 4C.4

Levels	Index	Name of Districts
V. High	> 1	Jaipur, Kota, Udaipur
High	.5 to 1	Ajmer, Sri Ganganagar
Medium	0 to .5	Bhilwara, Jodhpur, Pali
Low	–.5 to 0	Alwar, Bharatpur, Bikaner, Bundi, Chittorgarh, Jhunjhunu, Nagor, Sawai Madhopur, Tonk
V. Low	–.9 to –.5	Banswara, Barmer, Churu, Dungarpur, Jaisalmer, Jalore, Jhalawar, Sikar, Sirohi

TABLE 4D.1: Net Irrigation in Rajasthan by sources

(Area in '000 Hectares)

Year	Wells & tube-wells	% of Total	Canals	% of Total	Tanks	% of Total	Others	% of Total	Total
1956-59	865	60.19	308	21.43	244	16.98	20	1.40	1437
1974-77	1479	56.86	878	33.76	218	8.38	26	1.00	2601
1977-78	1732	54.69	1119	35.33	245	7.74	71	2.24	3167
1978-79	1730	59.76	950	32.82	192	6.63	23	0.79	2895
1979-80	2090	63.20	981	29.66	214	6.47	22	0.67	3307
1980-81	1874	62.82	941	31.55	112	3.75	56	1.88	2983
1981-82	1827	62.93	946	32.59	85	2.93	45	1.55	2903
1982-83	1997	62.06	1025	31.85	143	4.44	53	1.65	3218

Source: Rajasthan Statistical Abstract 1983, Directorate, Statistics and Economics, Jaipur.

TABLE 4D.2: Irrigation by Tube-Wells: A Declining Trend

Year	No. of Tube-wells	Per cent increase	Area irrigated ('000 ha)	Per cent variation (decline)	% of net irrigated area
1979-80	183278	15.36	270	—	8.16
1980-81	207435	13.21	246	–8.88	8.25
1981-82	232905	12.28	201	–18.29	6.92
1982-83	244219	4.86	176	–12.44	5.47
1983-84	255942	4.80	145	–17.61	4.00

A gradual decrease in net area irrigated by tube-wells is closely linked with constraint of power on the one hand and depletion in water-table, on account of continuous droughts, on the other hand. Farmers have become aware and conscious of the benefits of irrigation. They tend to increase and improve their irrigation facilities. Obviously, the number of energised wells have shown a gradual increase in terms of electric-connections. Farmers have their wells connected with transmission lines, but no sufficient electric flow in wires, with the fact that a power cut of 80 per cent has been imposed on big industries to supply power to the agricultural sector in daily rotation of 8 hours.

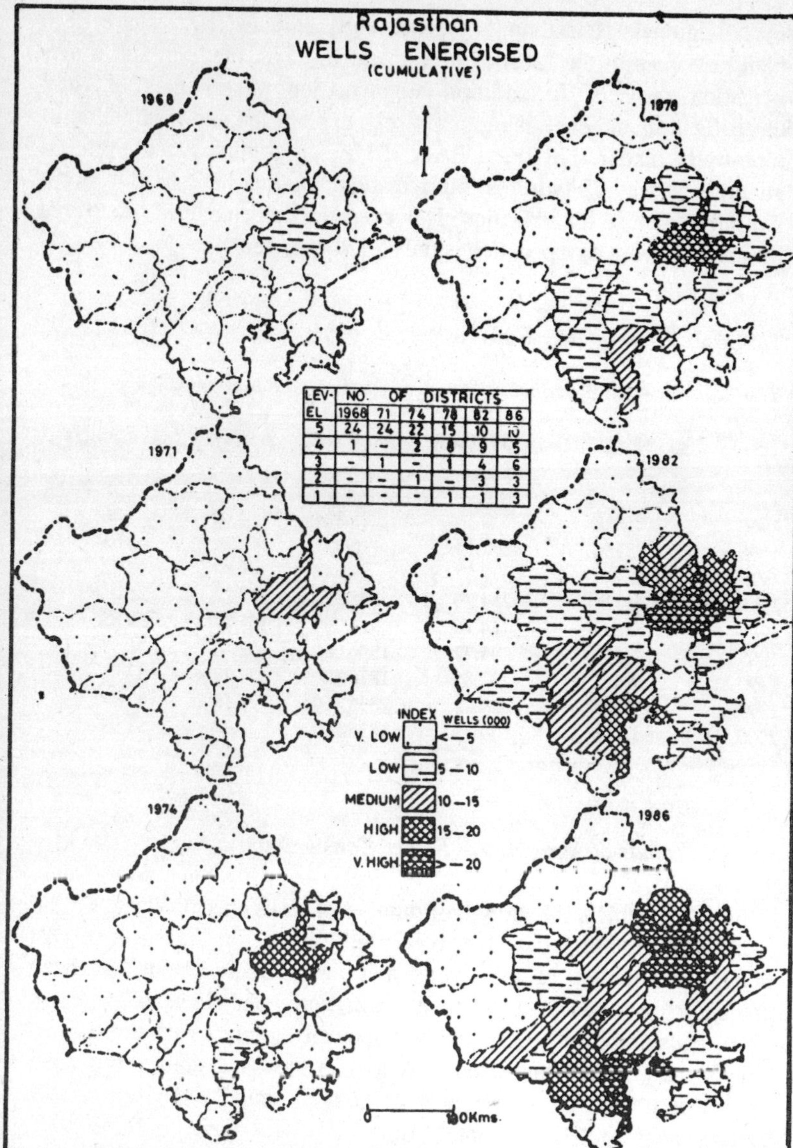

LEVEL	NO. OF DISTRICTS 1968	71	74	78	82	86
5	24	24	22	15	10	10
4	1	–	2	8	9	5
3	–	1	–	1	4	6
2	–	–	1	–	3	3
1	–	–	–	1	1	3

FIG. 4D.1

Irrigation, in Rajasthan, has consistently attracted large share from plan resources in the form of investment in large, medium and minor irrigation projects. In addition augmentation of schemes of rural electrification and energising pump-sets, exploration and installation of tube-wells under NREP, DPAP, DDP programmes and modest attempts by way of hydrums, lift irrigation, together have tried to boost the infrastructure for irrigation. However, the percentage of gross area irrigated to gross cropped area is only 21.26 per cent.

TABLE 4D.3: Power Consumption Trends

Year	Wells Electrified		Power consumption		
	No. of wells	% Growth	mkWh	% Growth	% of State's Total
1960	1038	—	3.824	—	7.06
1965	3759	262.14	10.055	162.94	2.65
1970	25470	577.57	89.644	791.54	11.42
1975	85323	234.99	345.330	285.22	22.04
1980	183238	114.76	916.040	165.27	30.85
1985	272880	48.92	1396.080	52.40	31.83
1990	362522	32.85	1876.120	34.38	32.42
1995	452164	24.73	2356.160	25.59	32.78
2000	541806	19.83	2836.200	20.37	33.03

Growth Trends of Agricultural Power Consumption

Table 4D.3 depicts the growth of number of wells energised since 1960 as well as growth attained in power utilisation. On the basis of past trend, the number of tube-wells and power requirement has been predicted up to AD 2000. There were nearly one thousand wells in 1960, consuming only 3.8 mkWh of power, merely seven per cent of State's total; which increased near to 273 thousand consuming 1396 mkWh of power, 31.18 per cent of State's total. By the turn of the century near to 542 thousands tube-wells will have to have 2836 mkWh of power, the quantum equal to power-consumption of Jaipur city for seven years and that of Ganganagar for 80 years, keeping in view the power statistics of 1987.

TABLE 4D.4: Per-well Availability of Power (in kWh)

Year	Annual	Monthly	Daily	Hourly
1960	3684	307.0	10.093	.421
1965	2675	223.0	7.329	.305
1970	3520	293.3	9.644	.402
1975	4047	337.3	11.088	.462
1980	4999	416.6	13.696	.571
1985	5116	426.3	14.017	.584
1990	5175	431.3	14.178	.591
1995	5211	434.2	14.276	.595
2000	5235	436.3	14.342	.598

Rajasthan is the driest State in India. The annual average rainfall varies from 90 cm in the Chambal basin to 13 cm in the Thar desert. Eleven districts of the State lie in the arid of semi-arid zone and these cover more than 61 per cent of the geographical area and 36 per cent of its total population. In the desert region, every second year is a dry year. Table 4D.1 reveals that the net irrigated area of the State was 1437 thousand hectares in 1956-59 which increased to 3218 thousand hectares in 1982-83 forming 12 and 21.26 per cent of the net area sown in the two respective periods. Well is the main source of irrigation in the State, on which more than sixty per cent of net irrigated area depends. Per-well periodic availability of power as shown in Table 4D.4, depicts a gradual increase in annual, monthly and daily power utility of a tube-well in Rajasthan. But it is not enough. A 5 horse-power motor[6] needs 3.731 kWh of power to pump water out of a well for an hour, while power availability for a well in Rajasthan is less than 0.600 kWh per hour.

The short fall in supply can be remedied by proper planning and management of existing power system and encouraging alternative sources of conventional power. The Solar Photovoltaic Water Pumping System can be used for both agricultural and community drinking water uses. The system can be operated during the sunshine hours of the day. Rajasthan is richly endowed with the solar energy. On an average, it receives insolation of 6 kWh per square metre per day for over 300 days per year. This is an enormous amount of energy that should be used for well irrigation in Rajasthan.

Levels of Energy Input to Agriculture in Rajasthan

The modification in agricultural sector can largely be understood through changes in agricultural energy consumption behaviour, for which it is necessary to compute the rate of shift from animate to inanimate source of power so as to reckon the degree of agricultural revolution. An attempt has been made here to identify the levels of energy input to agriculture at district level in Rajasthan for two points of time during 1971-72 and 1981-82 (Fig. 4D.2). Energy input to agriculture in Rajasthan, in term of animate power consisting of cattle, buffaloes, camel and man, on the one hand, and in terms of inanimate power consisting mechanical implements i.e. tractors, oil-engine, pump-sets and crushers on the other hand, have been taken into consideration. To analyse and evaluate the quantum of energy implemented towards agricultural activities in the State under the animate and inanimate heads, actual number of variables have been converted into HP values, on the basis of table suggested by IGU commission (Table 4D.5).

TABLE 4D.5: Conversion of Animate and Inanimate Forms of Energy into H.P. Values

Per animate variable	H.P. value	Per inanimate variable	H.P. value
Man	0.2	Pump-set	5.0
Cattle	0.5	Oil-engine	5.0
Buffalo	0.9	Crusher	7.5
Camel	2.0	Tractor	50.0

Source: I.G.U. Commission, 1974.

District-wise percentage of animate and inanimate forms of energy has been calculated so as to find out the levels of energy input (Table 4D.6). Gross growth of energy consumption over the decade is also calculated. Only seven districts, namely, Alwar, Bharatpur, Jaipur, Jalore, Pali, Sawai Madhopur and Sirohi, exhibited gross growth above the State-average 59.39 per cent during 1972-82. Only Jaisalmer district experienced a decrease of 4.75 per cent, reducing its aggregate consumption from 526 HP in 1972 to 501 HP in 1982, and the situation is more worse today. Almost 99 per cent energy for agriculture in Jaisalmer came from animate sources in 1972 which was still 92 per cent in 1982.

The most striking feature revealed in Table 4D.6, is that the percentage of animate form of energy declined in every district, increasing the percentage of inanimate form of energy. Even in

Jaisalmer district, where merely 1.33 per cent inanimate energy was utilised in 1971-72, it rose to 8.18 per cent in 1981-82. Moreover, Bikaner district showed a tremendous increase of inanimate power over the decade, rising from 0.66 per cent in 1972 to 18.72 per cent in 1982. A more clear picture of the growth of inanimate form of power to agriculture in Rajasthan, is depicted in Table 4D.7.

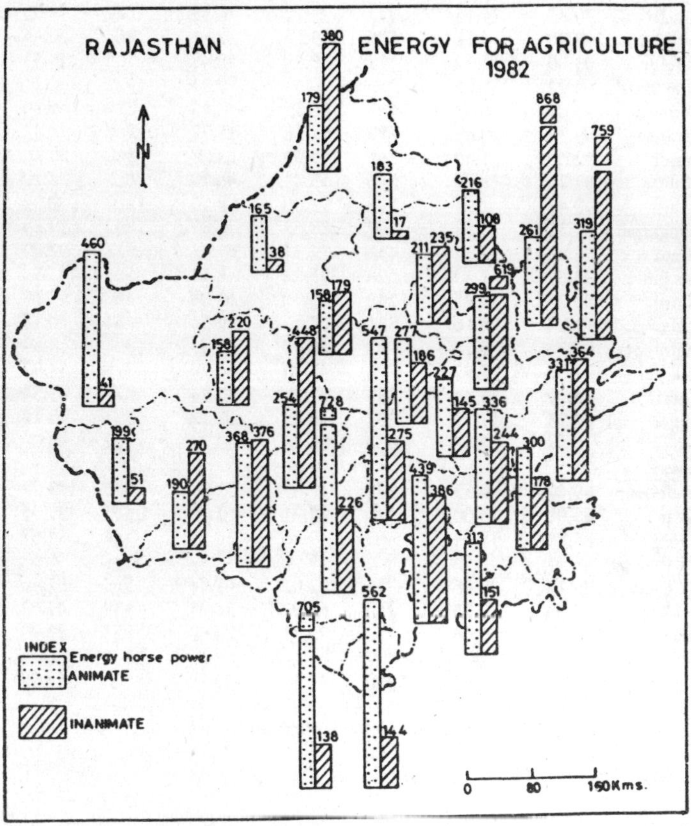

FIG. 4D.2

TABLE 4D.6: Energy Input to Agriculture in Terms of Animate and Inanimate Forms of Energy

(per '000 Hectares)

Sl. No.	District	Energy input in 1971-72			Energy input in 1981-82			Gross growth over the decade in %
		Animate %	Inanimate %	Total HP	Animate %	Inanimate %	Total HP	
1.	Ajmer	89.78	10.22	323	59.83	40.17	463	43.34
2.	Alwar	70.87	29.13	412	23.12	76.88	1129	174.03
3.	Banswara	95.90	4.10	586	79.55	20.45	704	20.14
4.	Barmer	93.09	6.22	193	79.60	20.40	250	29.53
5.	Bharatpur*	64.94	35.06	282	29.59	70.41	1078	282.27
6.	Bhilwara	93.09	6.91	608	66.55	33.45	822	35.20
7.	Bikaner	99.34	0.66	182.2	81.28	18.72	203	11.42
8.	Bundi	92.60	7.40	365	57.93	42.07	580	58.90
9.	Chittor	87.73	12.27	546	53.21	46.79	825	51.10
10.	Churu	98.47	1.53	196	91.50	8.50	200	2.04
11.	Dungarpur	97.31	2.69	707	83.63	16.37	843	19.24
12.	Jaipur	66.88	33.12	465	32.57	67.43	918	97.42
13.	Jaisalmer	98.67	1.33	526	91.82	8.18	501	(—)4.75
14.	Jalore	80.25	19.75	238	36.96	63.04	460	93.28
15.	Jhalawar	91.84	8.16	331	67.46	32.54	464	40.18
16.	Jhunjhunu	91.84	8.16	282	66.67	33.33	324	14.89
17.	Jodhpur	70.08	29.92	244	41.80	58.20	378	54.92
18.	Kota	86.79	13.21	333	62.76	37.24	478	43.54
19.	Nagor	82.28	17.72	237	46.88	53.12	337	42.19
20.	Pali	76.54	23.46	358	36.18	63.82	702	96.09
21.	Sawai Madhopur	89.47	10.53	342	47.63	52.37	695	103.22
22.	Sikar	85.00	15.00	320	47.31	52.69	446	39.38
23.	Sirohi	85.86	14.14	403	49.46	50.54	744	84.62
24.	Sri Ganganagar	70.14	29.86	355	32.02	67.98	559	57.46
25.	Tonk	92.06	7.94	252	61.02	38.98	372	47.62
26.	Udaipur	94.94	5.06	770	76.31	23.69	954	23.90
	Rajasthan	83.03	16.97	330	49.62	50.38	526	59.39

* Dholpur was separated from Bharatpur in 1981. Hence included in Bharatpur.

TABLE 4D.7: Growth of Inanimate Energy over Animate Energy

Form of Energy		Year H.P.	1971-72 %	Year H.P.	1981-82 %	Variation H.P.	over decade %
I.	Animate	4603128.6	82.89	4846692	49.62	243563.4	5.29
	Human	1063961.2	19.16	1439178	14.74	375216.8	35.27
	Animal	3539167.4	63.73	3407514	34.88	–131653.4	–3.73
II	Inanimate	950222.5	17.11	4921699	50.38	3971476.5	417.95
Aggregate		5553351.1	100.00	9768391	100.00	4215039.9	75.90

Table 4D.7 reveals that the use of animal power decreased by 3.72 per cent, while use of manpower increased by 35.27 per cent during 1971-72 and 1981-82. Thus, the total increase of animate power was only 5.29 per cent as against the growth of 418 per cent in the inanimate form of power. Aggregate growth exhibited during the period was of the order of 75.9 per cent in Rajasthan. The use of inanimate form of power registered an excellent growth, which indicates the rate of shift from traditional style of agriculture towards mechanized form of cultivation.

Levels of Mechanization of Agriculture in Rajasthan

Maps and tables illustrate the fact that alike its physio-cultural disparities, the State of Rajasthan registered a high degree of variation in term of animate and inanimate energy input. All the districts are categorised into five levels concluding the fact that high level districts in terms of animate energy input reflect subsistence type of agriculture and low level districts rather more mechanized. Whereas in term of inanimate energy input high level districts are more mechanized than that of low level districts. Table 3D.8 displays the number of districts falling under five levels of energy input and more clear picture is illustrated in maps (Figs. 4D.3 and 4D.4).

Energy Input to Agriculture in Western Rajasthan

Western Rajasthan part of the Indian desert extends over an area of 1,88,177 sq km covering 55 per cent area and 33 per cent population in ten districts with an average density of 61 person per km. The geographical location lies between 24°40′–28°40′ North Latitude and 69°30′-76°5′ East Longitudes, forming its physical frame by aridity and sand. Basically, this is an agricultural and rural region having no major geological resources, less variety of relief, soil, vegetation and cultural landscape, low water availability and far less density of population than that of State and national average. The sparse population and low standard of living are its main characteristics endowed by recurrent famines, drought and epidemics. Out of total population of this region (115 lakh), about 80 per cent is involved in agriculture and animal husbandry. Both man and animal have been intensively engaged in formulating the cultural landscape of this region. So, the extensive use of animate energy has always been the

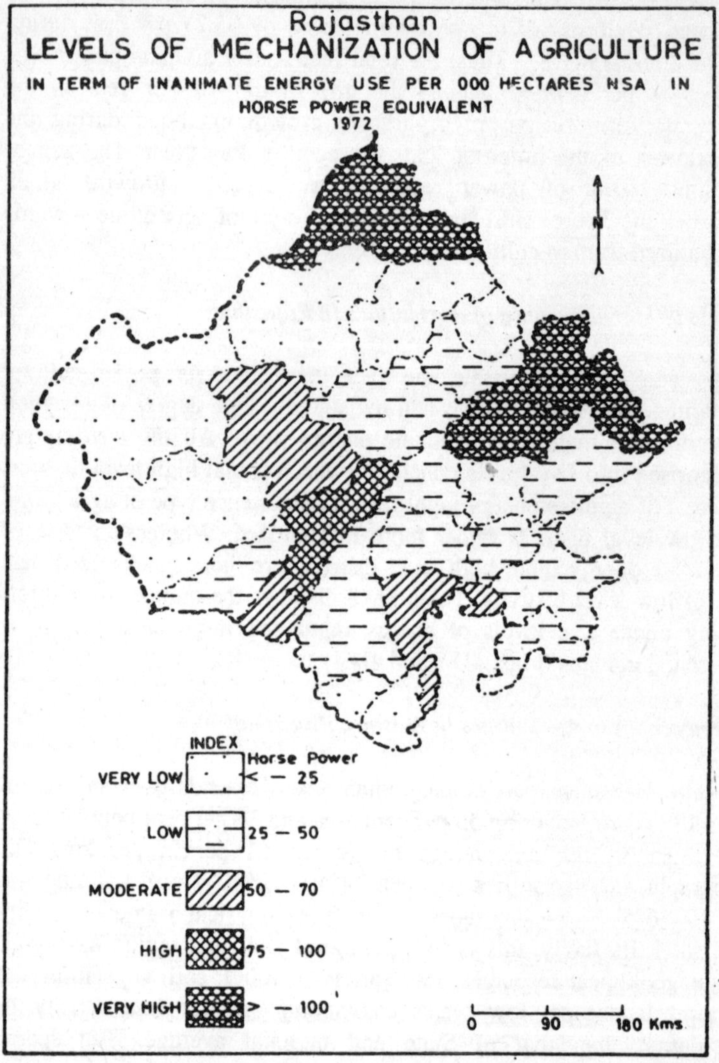
Rajasthan
LEVELS OF MECHANIZATION OF AGRICULTURE
IN TERM OF INANIMATE ENERGY USE PER 000 HECTARES NSA IN HORSE POWER EQUIVALENT
1972
N
INDEX
Horse Power
VERY LOW < — 25
LOW 25 — 50
MODERATE 50 — 70
HIGH 75 — 100
VERY HIGH > — 100
0 90 180 Kms

FIG. 4.D.3

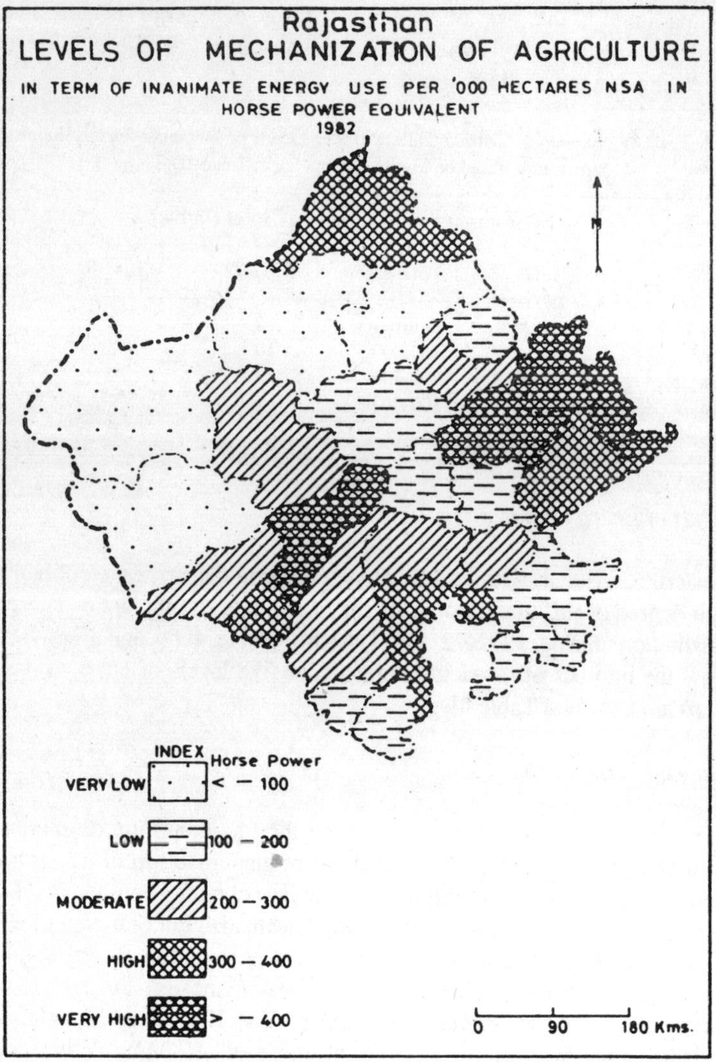
Rajasthan
LEVELS OF MECHANIZATION OF AGRICULTURE
IN TERM OF INANIMATE ENERGY USE PER '000 HECTARES NSA IN HORSE POWER EQUIVALENT
1982
N
INDEX
Horse Power
VERY LOW < — 100
LOW 100 — 200
MODERATE 200 — 300
HIGH 300 — 400
VERY HIGH > — 400
0
90
180 Kms.

FIG. 4D.4

most important factor in developing the agricultural practice of this region in particular and of Rajasthan as well as India, in general. Comparatively, the use of inanimate form of energy is still less important even today when the mechanization of agriculture is increasing at a tremendous speed.

TABLE 4D.8: Number of Districts Falling Under Levels of Inanimate Energy Input to Agriculture Based on Figures Computed in Table 4D.6

Levels	Horse Power		No. of Districts	
	1971-72	1981-82	1971-72	1981-82
Very Low	Below 25	Below 100	8	4
Low	25-50	100-200	10	8
Medium	50-75	200-300	3	6
High	75-100	300-400	1	4
Very High	Above 100	Above 400	4	4

Levels of Energy Input

Western Rajasthan, with its less physio-cultural disparities, exhibited a high degree of differentiation in terms of animate and inanimate energy distribution during 1971-72 and 1981-82. Table 4D.9 and Fig. 4D.5 show the number of districts falling under five levels of energy input, Maps are based on Table 4D.6.

Relevant Observation

Farmers in Rajasthan, tend to shift from the traditional use of animate form of energy towards an advanced use of inanimate sort of power but their socio-economic conditions and physio-climatic hurdles prevent them, check their shifting mood towards mechanization of agriculture.

Western Rajasthan is endowed with less physio-climatic variations, but there exists a great deal of disparities in the use the means of energy required for agricultural practice. The HP values of animate variables vary from 0.2 to 2.0 HP and those of inanimate variables it vary from 5 HP to 50 HP. There is ten times intra-variables variation for individual form of energy and 25 times variation in between animate and inanimate form of energy.

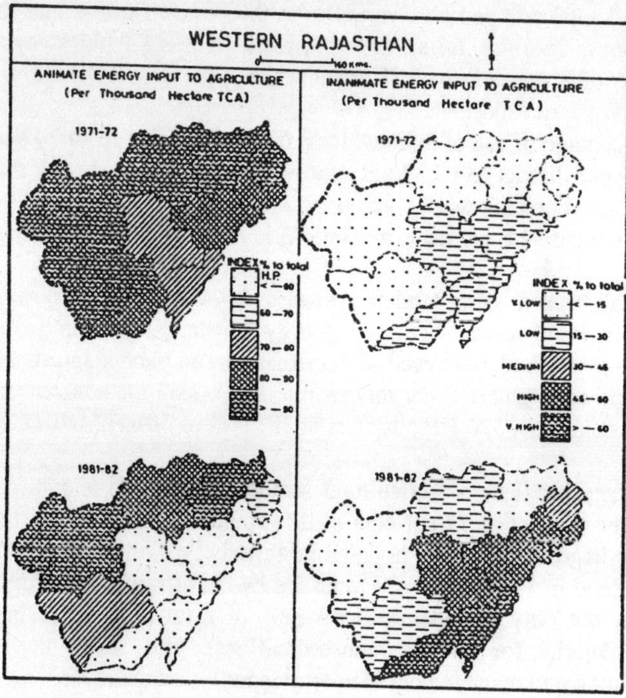

FIG. 4D.5

TABLE 4D.9: Number of Districts Falling Under Level of Energy Input to Agriculture Based on Figures Computed in Table 4D.6.

Levels	Animate energy		Inanimate energy	
	1971-72	1981-82	1971-72	1981-82
Very Low	Nil	5	6	2
Low	Nil	1	4	2
Moderate	2	1	Nil	1
High	3	1	Nil	3
Very High	5	2	Nil	2

Inter-district agricultural inanimate share of power consumption per thousand total cropped area varied from 0.6 per cent in Bikaner to 29.9 per cent in Jodhpur during 1971-72, while, it was 8.2 per cent in Jaisalmer to 63.8 per cent in Pali district during the year 1981-82, in the case of Western Rajasthan.

The percentage of use of animate form of power varied from 70 per cent in Jodhpur district to 99.37 per cent in Bikaner district during the year 1971-72, whereas it was experienced 23.12 per cent (minimum) in Alwar district and 91.8 per cent (maximum) in Jaisalmer district during 1981-82.

There has been a rising tendency towards inanimate use of power and a falling trend towards animate energy consumption. The gross energy consumption also showed an increasing trend except Jaisalmer district where aggregate HP per thousand total cropped area decreased by 4.75 per cent from 526 HP pth/TCA in 1971-72 to 501 HP pth/TCA in 1981-82.

The energy problem of agricultural sector in Rajasthan should be studied in the context of 79 per cent of its population living in 34,968 inhabited villages. The rural population is expected to grow from 27122 thousand in 1981 to 4,94,30 thousand by the turn of the century. Agriculture, not only provides jobs for bulk of rural population, but also, raw material for various industries. Hence, this sector needs proper planning and management of energy input.

4E. Power Consumption Pattern in Water Supply

Water is the prime sustainer of organic-life. Most prominent civilizations have flourished on river banks. Rajasthan is not blessed with enough perennial rivers. Hence, the State depends on Monsoon and underground water for its drinking and irrigation water requirements. The main problem of the region is inadequate and erratic rainfall which cause frequent scarcity conditions resulting in migration of men and livestock within and outside the State. The State Government has geared up its entire machinery to face the challenge of this year's water crisis, the worst ever faced by the State during past many years. With the steps already taken and the new ones under execution, the authorities hope to successfully tide over the prevailing critical situation. On the new steps, apart from the digging of new tube-wells, deepening of existing tube-wells, hiring of private tube-wells and wells, installation of hand pumps and supplying water through tankers, initiated by the Government is alcohol spray on lakes in a bid to stop evaporation of water. This new technique was tried in Jaipur during 1986 when cetyle steryl alcohol was sprayed on Ramgarh Lake at its different water levels. The Public Health Engineering Department hopes to try it again this year on lakes which have adequate quantity of water in them.

By the end of March 1987, 26,301 villages out of 34968 inhabited villages in the State, have been made available drinking water. During 1986-87, 2027 villages against the target of 1600 villages have been linked with various types of drinking water supply facilities. The Public Health Engineering Department hopes to link another 1200 villages with drinking water supply sources during the current financial year. As many as seventy six thousand handpumps have also been installed all over the State to make available drinking water to the people. Other steps taken by the Department included commissioning of 96 tube-wells, recommissioning of 175 old wells, laying of 718 km long pipelines and deepening of 270 wells. The Department has also provided drinking water supply facilities in as many 5,898 localities to scheduled castes and tribes. To tackle the water crisis last year, the Government had spent a total of Rs. 97 crores, and a contingency plan of Rs. 100 crores has been drawn up for implementation during the current financial year. There is a provision of Rs. 45 crores available in the State's budget for 1987-88 as against the out lay of Rs. 28.75 crores during the last financial year.

To maintain and augment the existing facilities of water supply an adequate amount of power is required. Table 4E.1 shows that there were only 277 water supply consumers in 1960 consuming only less than 13 mkWh of power, which rose to 7,228 at the end of March 1985 consuming more than 218 mkWh of power. Maximum growth of the order of 130 per cent was recorded in 1974-75 over the year 1969-70 when there were 813 water-suppliers in the State which rose to 1876 during five years period. The number of water-supply consumers is estimated to reach the figure 19021 by the turn of the century.

Table 4E.2 displays the trend of power-consumption by water-supply consumers since 1959-60 to 1984-85. Short-term fore cast on the basis of past trend has been made up to AD 2000. The table depicts that the percentage of aggregate power consumption, under the head of water-supply consumers, has been gradually declining. This is proved by the fact that 6.19 per cent of total power consumption was utilised in water-supply system, reduced to 4.49 per cent at the end of

March 1980. The percentage of total power consumption showed a slight increase in 1985, consuming 4.98 per cent of State's total power. Maximum increase of power consumption was exhibited during 1965-70, of the order of 124 per cent over five years' period, due to greater emphasis given by the authorities, on the improvement of drinking water facilities. It is estimated that near about 473 million kWh of power will be required by water supply consumers in the year of AD 2000 which is more than the double that of the present requirement of power for the system.

TABLE 4E.1: Growth Trends of Water-Supply Consumers in Rajasthan

Year	Consumers	% of Total	Variation	% Variation
1959-60	277	0.38	—	—
1964-65	584	0.32	307	110.83
1969-70	813	0.27	229	39.21
1974-75	1876	0.27	1063	130.75
1979-80	3279	0.29	1421	75.75
1984-85	7228	0.40	3931	119.23
1989-90	12427	0.47	5199	71.93
1994-95	16358	0.48	3931	31.63
1999-2000	20289	0.49	3931	24.03

TABLE 4E.2: Growth Trends of Water-Supply Power-Consumption in Rajasthan (1959-60 to 1999-2000)

Year	mkWh	% of Total	Variation	% Variation
1959-60	12.676	23.41	—	—
1964-65	23.506	6.19	10.830	85.44
1969-70	52.635	6.70	29.129	123.92
1974-75	83.800	5.36	31.165	59.21
1979-80	133.348	4.49	49.548	59.13
1984-85	218.316	4.98	84.968	63.72
1989-90	303.284	5.23	84.968	38.92
1994-95	388.252	5.39	84.968	28.02
1999-2000	473.220	5.51	84.968	21.88

District-wise Water Supply Consumption

District-wise distribution of power consumption in water supply system has been shown in appendix Table 4E.3 by mkWh and percentage of State's total for three points of time viz., 1979-80,

1984-85, and 1989-90. The power distribution is grossly imbalanced. The table reveals that three districts consumed around the average of the State on the basis of percentage of the total, while seven districts remained above the average and sixteen districts below the average during 1984-85. The picture is almost the same in preceding and coming five years. Ajmer, Barmer, Bikaner, Churu, Jaipur, Jodhpur and Kota districts showed above the average, Nagor, Sri Ganganagar and Udaipur districts consumed average power and rest of the sixteen districts remained below the district average in terms of percentage of total power used in water supply in the State during 1984-85. Jaipur district alone consumed as much power as 20 per cent of the State's total, followed by Ajmer (12%), Jodhpur (11.5%), Bikaner (7%), Kota (6.8%), Churu (4.5%) and Barmer (4.4%) districts. These seven districts accounted almost 67 per cent of State's total power-utilization for water supply, while they constituted only 32.8 per cent State's human population and 33.25 per cent of livestock in an area of 38 per cent of the State. Remaining 20 districts, however survived on 33 per cent of State's power for water-supply purpose for their 67 per cent State's population of man and animal each, spread over an area of 62 per cent of the State.

Geography has beset Rajasthan with the biggest problem of taming and colonising the inhospitable terrains, exploring and exploiting the life giving water-resources. The strategy required to be adopted for tackling the problem of water-deficit, include maximum utilisation of rain water and underground water. A great deal of power on the water-supply system improvement is required keeping in view the sinking water-table and erratic rain-fall. How the State is meeting out this challenging task is a saga of our own times.

The water crisis has taken not only the country side in its grip but also big towns like Jaipur, Ajmer, Kishangarh, Beawar, Jodhpur, Udaipur and Bharatpur are facing water deficit problem. The worst among them are Ajmer and Beawar where water is being supplied once in three days. The department is trying to maintain the enhanced supply of 72 lakh gallons of water a day to Ajmer city. The supply has been raised from 52 lakh gallons a day by digging more tube-wells installing more handpumps. Besides, drinking water is being supplied to Ajmer and Beawar towns through water tanks.

The pink city of Jaipur is being supplied water from Ramgarh lake and 352 tube-wells. In Ramgarh lake, the water level after the monsoon season was 45.5 feet in 1986 as against 52.8 feet in 1985 and

42.9 feet in 1984. Its full capacity is 60 feet. The pink city is being supplied 365 lakh gallons of water per day including 29 lakh gallons from lake Ramgarh. The lake's present level is 33.6 feet and since 1.6 feet of water is drawn from it every month the authorities hope to continue the supply from it till end of June 1988. In addition to 352 existing tube-wells the Department will dig 60 new tube-wells to meet the situation. During 1986-87, the power consumed by these 352 tube-wells was of the order of 33.418 mkWh, sharing near about 95 thousand units of power by one tube-well, which accounts 260 kWh per day. Hence, additional new sixty tube-wells will require another load of 15,616 kWh of power per day and 5.7 million kWh for the coming year.

The situation in Udaipur and Jodhpur towns is also being met by sinking more tube-wells and handpumps. To augment the supply to Bharatpur, Deeg and Nagar towns, a scheme to lift the dead water from bandh besides sinking of tube-wells, has been worked out. Likewise, the problem of Jodhpur city is sought to be met with the help of Jodhpur Lift Scheme on the Indira Gandhi Canal.

According to Health Engineering Department, in the desert districts, 76 tankers are supplying drinking water to 528 villages with a population of 2.5 lakh. Thirty-one camel carts are also being utilised for transporting water in 21 remote villages of Bikaner district. In addition subsidy is being given for drawing water from 246 deep wells for the benefit of 1.77 lakh people. Every effort being made to meliorate the situation in the State, will require additional amount of energy, and this will create a big power-deficit ahead.

4F. Power Consumption in Street Lighting

The growth of street lighting load is a function of population growth which is directly related to the length of roads and streets of cities and towns and to some extent of villages. The load also depends on the total revenue and the capacity of the municipality or Panchayat Samitis to pay for the amenity. Installation of 40 watt bulbs in the streets of electrified villages are found satisfactory for public illumination. Whereas, a high voltage illumination is found necessary along the roads of urban centres. Obviously, the public lighting in urban areas shared from three to seven times higher power consumption than that in rural areas since 1970. The number of rural-street-lighting consumers increased by 288 per cent as against 95 per cent growth of urban street-lighting consumers during past ten years. Moreover, out of 20 thousand electrified villages, only 3,622 villages shared 23 per cent of total street-lighting power consumption in Rajasthan. Whereas, out of 201 towns, 1162 urban consumers shared about 77 per cent of street-lighting power-consumption in the year ending March 1985.

TABLE 4F.1: Street Lighting Power Consumption Pattern in Urban and Rural Areas

Year	No. of Consumers		Power Consumption in mkWh			
	Urban	Rural	Urban	Sector	Rural	Sector
			mkWh	%	mkWh	%
1971	—	—	7.00	80.37	1.71	19.63
1972	—	—	8.09	82.38	1.73	17.62
1973	547	815	10.06	82.19	2.18	17.81
1974	554	884	9.87	82.25	2.13	17.75
1975	595	934	10.25	84.78	1.84	15.22
1976	643	1014	11.56	80.67	2.77	19.33
1977	679	1163	13.10	86.13	2.11	13.87
1978	751	1318	15.18	83.96	2.90	16.04
1979	783	1680	16.19	82.56	3.42	17.44
1980	851	1859	16.28	83.83	3.14	16.17
1981	885	2054	16.13	82.59	3.40	17.41
1982	919	2406	14.44	79.52	3.72	20.48
1983	958	2681	16.73	73.93	5.90	26.07
1984	1033	3007	18.45	76.37	5.71	23.63
1985	1162	3622	22.51	76.77	6.81	23.23

Table 4F.1 displays a segregated picture of urban and rural street-lighting consumption pattern of power as well as number of consumers. It is interesting to note that the rural sector had increased its share of street-lighting power from 15 per cent in 1975 to 26 per cent in 1983 due to greater emphasis given by authorities on rural electrification. But this share again declined to 23 per cent in 1984 and 1985, increasing the share of urban sector upto 77 per cent. The successive droughts have eroded the purchasing power of the people in 31,922 drought prone villages. Consequently, the paying capacity of village-Panchayats has also declined. Hence, there occurred a fall of 3 per cent in the rising trend of rural street lighting power consumption.

Growth trend of street-lighting power consumption pattern is shown in Table 4F.2, which reveals that there were only 25 street lighting consumers, consuming 2.15 mkWh of power in 1959-60. The number of consumers rose to 2710 at the end of March 1985, consuming 19.42 millions kWh of power. By the turn of the century the number of consumers is estimated more than 11 thousand and power consumption 56.298 mkWh.

The power consumption in street-lighting though increased from 2.15 mkWh in 1960 to 29.32 mkWh in 1985, its share in terms of percentage of total power utilisation in Rajasthan decreased from 3.97 per cent in 1959-60, to 0.67 per cent in 1984-85. Maximum growth of street lighting power consumption in the State was recorded during 1960-65 and 1975-80, making a rise of 218.14 per cent and 60.63 per cent in the respective periods.

TABLE 4F.2: Growth Trend of Street Lighting Power

Year	Consumers			Consumption		
	Number	% of total	% of growth	mkWh	% of total	% of growth
1960	25	0.03	—	2.15	3.97	—
1965	599	0.33	22.96	6.84	1.80	218.14
1970	913	0.31	52.42	8.60	1.09	25.73
1975	1529	0.22	67.47	12.09	0.77	40.58
1980	2710	0.22	77.24	19.42	0.68	60.63
1985	4784	0.30	76.53	29.32	0.67	50.98
1990	6858	0.26	43.35	38.31	0.66	30.66
1995	8932	0.27	30.24	47.30	0.65	23.47
2000	11006	0.27	23.22	56.29	0.65	19.01

District-wise Street Lighting Power Consumption

Table 4F.3 exhibits district-wise trends of street lighting power consumption for three points of time viz., 1979-80, 1984-85 and 1989-90. The street lighting power consumption was grossly imbalanced. During the year 1979-80, only five districts consumed as much share of street lighting power as an average of the State, 13 districts remained below the average and 8 districts above the average. The number of districts falling below the State's average rose to 15 during 1984-85 reducing the number of districts falling in the average category up to two and increased by one under above the average category. Only Nagor district was estimated as an average consumer, 15 districts below the Sate's average and 10 districts above the average in 1989-90.

TABLE 4F.3: Spatial Street Lighting Power Consumption Trends

Distts.	1979-80		1984-85		1989-90	
	mkWh	% of Total	mkWh	% of Total	mkWh	% of Total
1. Ajmer	2.087	10.74	2.427	8.28	2.767	6.97
2. Alwar	0.454	2.34	0.811	2.77	1.168	2.94
3. Banswara	0.361	1.86	0.635	2.17	0.909	2.29
4. Barmer	0.214	1.10	0.227	0.77	0.240	0.60
5. Bharatpur	0.011	0.05	0.907	3.09	1.803	4.54
6. Bhilwara	0.920	4.74	1.820	6.21	2.720	6.85
7. Bikaner	0.970	4.99	0.922	3.14	0.900	2.27
8. Bundi	0.392	2.02	0.579	1.97	0.766	1.93
9. Chittor	0.859	4.42	1.515	5.17	2.171	5.47
10. Churu	0.728	3.75	1.469	5.01	2.210	5.56
11. Dungarpur	0.396	2.04	0.566	1.93	0.736	1.85
12. Jaipur	3.363	17.31	4.503	15.36	5.643	14.21
13. Jaisalmer	0.124	0.64	0.124	0.42	0.124	0.31
14. Jalore	0.108	0.55	0.121	0.41	0.134	0.34
15. Jhalawar	0.598	3.08	0.622	2.13	0.646	1.63
16. Jhunjhunu	0.234	1.20	0.175	0.60	0.200	0.50
17. Jodhpur	1.144	5.89	2.173	7.41	3.202	8.06
18. Kota	1.443	7.43	2.215	7.56	2.987	7.52
19. Nagor	0.449	2.32	0.714	2.43	1.384	3.48
20. Pali	0.608	3.13	0.792	2.70	0.976	2.46
21. S. Madhopur	0.620	3.19	0.742	2.53	0.864	2.17
22. Sikar	0.265	1.36	0.441	1.50	0.617	1.55
23. Sirohi	0.511	2.64	0.592	2.03	0.673	1.69
24. Sri Ganganagar	0.728	3.75	1.991	6.79	3.254	8.18
25. Tonk	0.389	2.00	0.464	1.58	0.539	1.36
26. Udaipur	1.450	7.46	1.771	6.04	2.092	5.27
Total	19.426	100.00	29.318	100.00	39.725	100.00
<3%		13		15		15
3-4%		5		2		1
>4%		8		9		10

NOTES

1. Kusumlata Taneja, *Morphology of Indian Cities*.
2. INDIA, Basic Economic Information 1986 by Agrawal, Verma, Gupta.

3. Budget-Study-1986-87, Directorate of Economics and Statistics, Rajasthan, Jaipur.
4. Dholpur is included with Bharatpur district
5. Budget Study 1987-88.
6. One Kilowatt hour is equal to 1.34 hours-power, The Energy Question by Gerald Foley pp. 334.

5

URBAN POWER CONSUMPTION PATTERN IN RAJASTHAN

IT IS a rationale approach to assess the use of power in urban centres, because towns and cities in Rajasthan are consuming nearly fifty per cent of its available power, where hardly 21 per cent of its total population. Thus the correlation of percentage of power consumption with the population-distribution in Rajasthan is not very significant. The urban use shared 76 per cent of the State's power-consumption in 1970-71 which reduced to 47.96 per cent in 1980-81 due to greater emphasis on rural-electrification. The percentage of urban power-consumption again rose to 52.21 per cent in 1984-85 reducing the share of rural sector to 47.79 per cent for 79 per cent rural population of the State.

There has been a decreasing trend in the share of urban power consumption. This is evident by the fact that according to 1971 Census 76 per cent power was consumed by 17.6 per cent population of the State which declined by 28 per cent reducing the share up to 48 per cent for 21 per cent urban population as per 1981 Census. The share of urban population has increased while the share of urban power consumption has decreased over the decade. This trend will tend to minimize the variation in distribution of power between urban and rural sectors of the State. Table 6A.3 given in Chapter 6, illustrates the power variations between urban and rural sectors.

The urban sector in Rajasthan, consists of 201 towns and cities of varying population size have a variety of functions. According to the size of population, these urban centres are categorised into five groups.

Population Size	*No. of Towns*
Below 5000	1
5000– 9999	25
10000 – 19999	101

20000 – 49999	52
50000 – 99999	11
Above 100000	11

A comparison of power and population reveals the following picture in Rajasthan (Table 5.1).

TABLE 5.1: Comparison of Power and Population

Year	Urban population ('000)	Per cent of State's total	Urban power in mkWh	Per cent of State's total	Per Capita power con-consumption (kWh)
1971	4544	17.64	728.69	75.99	160.36
1981	7211	21.05	1404.86	47.96	194.82
1982	7329	20.93	1505.45	48.08	205.41
1983	7529	20.98	1490.70	45.60	197.99
1984	7795	21.17	2055.24	49.54	263.66
1985	8068	21.35	2290.09	52.21	283.85
1986	8348	21.54	2467.97	51.33	295.64

It is interesting to note that having less than 22 per cent of State's total population the urban sector has been consuming more than 50 per cent of State's total power budget obviously because of urban areas' multi-dimensional functions and activities.

Cities do not only serve the population of its own providing them with a variety of functions and facilities viz. domestic, commercial, industrial, educational, administrative and so on, but they also attract and serve the rural population simultaneously. An adequate and stable supply of power is needed to operate various functions associated with cities. The urban functions of Rajasthan are classified in seven categories on the basis of availability of data. Percentage of total urban power consumption for each of the functional sectors is computed since 1970-71, so as to assess the requirement of power for a particular function.

The urban power distribution pattern in Rajasthan among seven types of functional categories during the period 1970-71/1985-86 is given by percentage of total urban consumption in Table 5.2. The table shows that more than 60 per cent of urban power is consumed by industrial sector and rest of the 40 per cent is distributed among remaining six sectors. Though the percentage of total urban power has decreased yet the volume of the consumption under industrial sector has increased. The urban power consumption under domestic sector shows increasing trend both in terms of units and percentage of total. Rest of the urban functional sectors have shown marginal changes in terms of percentage of total power utilization in urban centres of Rajasthan. The variation in power distribution was recorded from one per cent to more than 60 per cent in street-lighting and industrial sectors respectively. The industrial sector always remained first order consumer of urban power, followed by domestic (II), commercial (III), water-supply (IV), agriculture (V), street-lighting (VI) and others (VIII).

TABLE 5.2: **Urban Power Distribution Pattern in Rajasthan (in percentage of total urban power consumption)**

Year	Indus. I	Dom. II	Comm. III	Water Spl. IV	Agrl. V	St Lt VI	Mix VII	Total mkWh	% of Rajasthan
1970-71	66.45	7.23	5.97	6.72	3.09	0.96	9.57	728.7	75.99
1971-72	67.26	7.76	6.52	5.97	4.34	1.01	7.13	802.1	72.63
1972-73	66.93	8.14	6.58	6.26	4.46	1.18	6.44	853.5	67.66
1973-74	64.79	9.08	6.76	7.26	5.05	1.17	5.89	842.1	63.24
1974-75	64.56	9.00	7.44	6.34	4.51	1.07	7.07	959.0	61.30
1975-76	68.56	8.93	7.30	5.96	3.76	1.03	4.46	1126.2	61.79
1976-77	67.96	8.89	7.34	5.89	3.63	1.03	5.27	1273.0	60.40
1977-78	67.61	9.87	7.67	6.03	3.42	1.13	4.27	1339.1	59.04
1978-79	68.14	9.62	7.47	5.65	3.87	1.57	4.20	1531.3	56.20
1979-80	63.77	11.12	8.04	6.25	5.35	1.10	4.37	1506.8	50.75
1980-81	59.69	13.03	8.92	7.03	4.79	1.15	5.39	1404.9	47.96
1981-82	57.87	13.89	9.26	6.66	6.09	0.96	5.27	1505.5	48.08
1982-83	53.04	15.93	10.74	7.50	6.04	1.12	5.62	1490.7	45.60
1983-84	62.74	13.13	8.23	5.73	4.75	0.89	4.50	2055.2	49.54
1984-85	59.20	13.96	8.49	6.55	6.40	0.98	4.41	2290.1	52.21
1985-86	60.06	—	—	—	4.27	—	—	2468.0	51.33

5A. Power Profile of Ganganagar City

Adequate supply of power is one of the basic needs of urban life. Present capacity of electricity available to Ganganagar city is not capable to meet the energy requirement. It needs to be augmented to bridge the gap between demand and supply and to meet the future need. This is an attempt to analyse the existing distribution pattern of power consumption and to evaluate growth trends of energy utilized in

Ganganagar during the past 12 years. All the relevant data regarding power and consumers have been taken from statistical records in the RSEB ExEn Office, Ganganagar. Data regarding population have been extracted from District Census Report of Ganganagar.

Supply Sources: Transmission and Distribution System

For the first four decades of this century people used to consume locally available traditional fuels in the then Ramnagar village and now 'Purani Abadi', the old part of Ganganagar town situated west of the 'a' minor. The 'a' minor, distributary of Gang Canal, divides the old and new planned part of Ganganagar. *Purani Abadi*, primarily a residential area, needs its power supply mainly for domestic lighting except the Jagatjeet Cotton Textile and a few scattered flour mills. While in eastern Ganganagar power is distributed in variety of functions.

In 1942, the generation of electricity commenced through a plan with the capacity of 2315 kilowatts hour near Sugar Mill. With the advent of Gang Canal, the town exhibited greater demand of power. Consequently, three turbo-sets (1000 + 750 + 565 kW), two steam sets (400 + 200 kW) and two diesel-sets (200 + 300 kW) of an aggregate installed capacity of 3414 kWh were established at the eastern periphery of the town. After the formation of Rajasthan State Electricity Board in July 1957, all the electricity undertakings were transferred to the Board. The first single circuit high tension transmission line of 66 kV was erected and energised in January 1960. There are, ar present, five transmission lines provided with electricity supply required to the city.

1. Muktsar-Ganganagar 66 kV single circuit high tension transmission line.
2. Hanumangarh-Ganganagar 33 kV single circuit transmission line along the road.
3. Hanumangarh-Ganganagar 33 kV single circuit transmission line along the railway track.
4. Padampur-Ganganagar 132 kV single circuit transmission line and
5. Padampur-Ganganagar 132 kV single circuit extra-high-tension transmission line.

It was expected that with the erection of 132 kV single circuit EHT transmission line the city would have a better power supply. But the scarcity of electricity is still experienced in the city. Above-mentioned transmission lines have been supplying nearly 32 million kWh of power every year since 1983 which is almost equivalent to the power consumed in street-lighting in entire Rajasthan. This quantum of power is distributed among its consumers through 99 sub-stations working in the city. Prototype obsolete transformers installed at these sub-stations are responsible for unreliable power supply. Secondly, interruption in supply is very common to its consumers as the power cuts from Punjab and failure of Rajasthan Atomic Plant is recurrent phenomenon. Eventually, the industrial, commercial and a few prosperous domestic consumers tend to have their own generating sets so as to meet the power shortage during the periods of power-cuts.

Growth Trends of Consumers

The growth of consumers of power in Ganganagar can be traced back prior to its emergence as a new town in 1931. Then it was a rural settlement called Ramnagar of about 1700 inhabitants in 1921. Two incidents influenced the growth of population. Firstly, with the advent of Gang Canal and its promotion as a new District Headquarter, the population increased five folds, to 10,000 in 1931 making a growth of 485 per cent over the decade. Secondly, 125.8 per cent rate of growth was registered during 1941-51 when the excessive increase was mostly due to the influx of refugees attracted to this town by the nearness of Pak border. Growth rate variations are shown in the Table 5A.1.

TABLE 5A.1: Growth Trends of Population

Year	Population	Variation	% Variation
1921	1,700	—	—
1931	9,943	8,243	484.88
1941	16,136	6,199	62.29
1951	36,437	20,301	125.81
1961	63,854	27,417	75.24
1971	90,042	26,188	41.01
1981	1,23,692	33,650	37.37
1991*	1,57,342	33,650	27.37
2001*	1,90,992	33,650	21.39

* = Projected population = a + bt = (56392 + 3365 . t)

Growth Trends of Power-Connections

The number of connections of electricity consumers in Ganganagar exhibited an over all increase during the period of past 12 years. Domestic connections remained highest throughout the period followed by commercial and industrial consumers. The domestic consumers registered 78 per cent growth whereas commercial and industrial consumers showed 45.5 per cent and 56.46 per cent growth respectively. Street and water supply consumers remained unchanged. The bulk consumers made an increase of four folds during the period of 12 years. If we look at the growth pattern of connections, the trends emerge as shown in Table 5A.2:

TABLE 5A.2: Consumers' Growth Trends 1975-86

Category of Consumers	No. of Connections		Per cent of Total		% Growth 1986/1975
	1975	1986	1975	1986	
Domestic	8,163	14,552	69.50	73.4	78.2
Commercial	3,219	4,684	27.40	23.6	45.5
Industrial	356	557	3.03	2.8	56.4
Street	1	1	—	—	—
Water Supply	1	1	—	—	—
Bulk	8	35	0.07	0.2	337.8
Total	11,748	19,830	100.00	100.0	68.8

Growth Trend of Power Consumption

The pattern of electricity consumption in Ganganagar city is totally dependent on its fluctuating supply. The trend of power consumption shown in Table 5A.3 reveals a considerable variation among its consumers. The overall trend shows an increase of 70.8 per cent in time series data for the period 1975-86.

The table shows that the domestic consumption increased by 168 per cent remaining the second largest consumer of power in the city. The first order industrial consumers made 30 per cent growth in power consumption. Street lighting (219.8%) and bulk consumers (1563%) made highest growth in consumption of electricity in the city.

TABLE 5A.3: Consumption Growth Trends (1975-86)

Category	Consumption mkWh		Per cent of Total		Per cent growth 1986/1975 (min-max)
	1975	1986	1975	1986	
I Industrial	13.141	17.107	67.7	50.3	30.18
II Domestic	3.316	8.895	15.9	26.2	168.2
III Commercial	2.279	4.673	10.9	13.8	105.04
IV Water Supply	0.810	0.752	3.9	2.3	67.00
V Street light	0.219	0.546	1.1.	1.6	219.81
VI Bulk	0.113	2.018	0.5	5.8	1563.00
Total	19.878	33.991	100.0	100.0	70.80

Power Distribution Pattern in Ganganagar

The distribution of consumption of power in Ganganagar among its consumers since 1975 shows that nearly 90 per cent of the total energy distributed in the city is consumed by industrial, domestic and non-domestic sectors. Remaining 10 per cent is distributed among rest of the consumers. Though declining as a percentage of total power distribution, consumption under industrial sector is increasing. The distribution of power varied from 68.6 per cent for industrial sector to 0.8 per cent for street lighting in 1977 and from 50.3 per cent to 1.6 per cent in 1986 for respective sectors. Hence the industrial sector is the first order consumer followed by (II) domestic, (III) commercial, (IV) water supply, (V) road light and (VI) other consumers. This is revealed in the Table 5A.4.

TABLE 5A.4: Power Distribution Pattern in Percentage

Year	I	II	III	IV	V	VI	mkWh	% growth
1975	67.7	15.9	10.9	3.9	1.1	0.5	19.898	—
1977	68.6	15.4	9.9	3.5	0.8	1.8	25.854	+29.93
1978	61.1	17.4	12.3	4.2	1.1	3.9	23.380	- 9.57
1979	66.7	14.9	10.2	3.8	0.9	3.5	30.275	+29.49
1980	63.3	16.8	11.5	3.3	1.1	4.0	27.487	- 9.21
1981	60.0	18.0	11.4	4.3	1.1	5.2	24.946	- 9.24
1982	60.3	17.9	11.2	4.2	0.9	5.5	27.316	+ 9.50
1983	49.4	22.0	14.7	5.1	1.7	7.1	26.195	- 4.10
1984	56.5	19.0	11.2	4.1	2.4	6.8	32.798	+25.21
1985	51.9	23.7	13.3	3.4	2.2	5.5	30.249	- 7.77
1986	50.3	26.2	13.8	2.3	1.6	5.8	33.991	+12.37

Sectoral Power Consumption in Ganganagar

(i) *Industrial Consumption* – Three categories of industries have been taken into consideration as shown in Table 5A.5:

(a) *Small Scale Industries:* They include *atta-chakkies*, oil mills, cottongins, Cording machines, *Dal* mills, Rice hullers, small workshops having connected load below 20 kW. These industries consume 8-10 per cent of industrial power consumption.

(b) *Medium Scale Industries:* They perform almost the same type of activities as the small scale industries. Their productive capacity is greater and connected load ranges between 25-100BHP. These industries consumed 8-14 per cent of the aggregate industrial power consumption.

(c) *Large Scale Industries:* Those industries connected with loads of 100 to 500 BHP are included in this category. They comprise, sugar, cotton, ginning, pressing, rice factories and textile industry. This category shared 75-83 per cent of the total power consumption by all industries of Ganganagar.

TABLE 5A.5: Segregation of Industrial Power Consumption

Year	Aggregate Industrial Consumption ('000 Kwh)	Small '000 Kwh	Scale Per cent	Medium '000 Kwh	Scale Per cent	Large '000 Kwh	Scale Per cent
1974-75	13141	1324	10.1	1869	14.2	9948	75.7
1976-77	17726	1598	8.9	1649	9.3	14479	81.8
1977-78	14295	1463	10.2	1169	8.2	11663	81.6
1978-79	20190	1674	8.2	1835	9.1	16681	82.7
1979-80	17406	1605	9.3	1491	8.5	14310	82.2
1980-81	14990	1488	9.9	1656	11.1	11846	79.0
1981-82	16475	1630	9.9	1978	12.0	12867	78.1

The industrial consumers in Ganganagar registered 30 per cent over all growth over 12 years on an annual growth rate of 0.61 per cent.[1]

(ii) *Domestic Consumption*: Residential land comprises a greater part (3.6 km^2) of the developed land area in the city than does any other single land-use type. Domestic consumers made a growth of 78.2 per cent in their number and 167 per cent growth in their consumption during 1975-86. Population size and living-style of residents and their per capita income determine the amount of domestic power consumption. Domestic power consumption in Ganganagar was seven times less than that in Jaipur during 1974-75 and remained 7 times less in 1986 due to difference in their size.

(iii) *Non-domestic Consumption*: All kinds of commercial uses such as shops, business houses, hotels, petrol-pumps, service-stations, auditoria, cinemas and places of worship, cover less than five per cent of the total developed area in Ganganagar. Major commercial centres lies in the planned part of the city. The commercial consumers showed an increase of 45.5 per cent in their number and 92.2 per cent in their consumption during the period under study. This sector remained at third place in terms of power consumption making a share of 10-14 per cent of total power used in Ganganagar throughout the period under consideration.

(iv) *Power Consumption in Water Supply*: God has not blessed the city with a river but credit goes to late Maharaja Gangasingh who linked the city with a perennial source of water supply in 1927. Ideally speaking, each household should have a separate water connection, but this is not possible as a large number of poors cannot afford the installation of taps in their homes. There are 10,160 houses provided with water connections and 390 public taps for poors. On account of evergrowing population the present water supply system is unable to keep pace with water demand of residents of Ganganagar. The augmentation of water-supply will require subsequent increase in power-supply. To operate the present water supply-system a load of 500 HP is required. The current quantum of water supply to the city is about 20 lacs gallons a day. The augmentation scheme will produce 45 lacs gallons a day which would require double the amount of power of the present quantum. The water supply department exhibited 219.8 per cent growth of power-consumption during 1975-86 and shared only 1.6 per cent of the total power utilised in the city.

(v) *Power Consumption in Street Lighting*: In can be considered that the planned part of the city has a greater share of land under roads and streets than that of Purani Abadi and the street lighting system is much more improved in the first than in the second. Since the advent of 66kV Transmission from Muktsar in 1960, the length of roads and streets lit by electricity have been increased. Overhead distribution lines have been replaced by the underground cables along the main roads to maintain the beauty of the city. Most modern street lighting poles have been erected in the middle of the main roads, while in the Purani Abadi there still exist murk prone muddy lanes. The city has exhibited substantial growth of power consumption in street lighting making a rise of 219.8 per cent during 1975-86. This sector shared 1-2 per cent of total power consumption in Ganganagar.

(vi) *Bulk Supply for Mix Load*: Railway station, Military Cantonments, BSF, hospitals, education institutions with hostels, cinemas, factories with residential colonies etc. have been considered under this sector. The category includes the supply for bona fide purposes of lighting, heating, pumping, street lighting and industrial up to a connected load of 500 HP. The number of bulk power consumers and consumption have rapidly increased. The number of bulk consumers rose by 27 from 8 in 1975 to 35 in 1986. Whereas the consumption increased by 1905 thousand kWh from 113 thousand kWh in 1975 to 2018 thousand kWh in 1986.

Power Projection for Ganganagar

The city of Ganganagar has witnessed a growth rate of 3.73 per cent per year on the basis of 12 years power consumption. The power projection of the city reveals the following picture (Table 5A.6).

Ganganagar is one of the important energy consumer in Rajasthan situated far away from State's power-generating plants. The city was initially linked with Bhakra Power System when the Ganganagar-Muktsar 66 kV High Tension Single Circuit Transmission Line was energized in 1960. Since then the city has experienced evergrowing need of power supply. The power consumption has increased by 14 million kWh from 19.9 mkWh in 1975 to 33.99 mkWh in 1986 at an annual growth rate of 3.73 per cent.

Electricity supply has helped to open new vistas of prosperity and happiness for the residents of Ganganagar. But recurrent interruptions in the supply of power is a big problem due to shortage of sensitive equipment and alternate feed supply, over-load, greater susceptibility to faults in supply system and the lack of co-ordination between concerned institutions. The problem can be remedied by erection of high tension transmission lines and stabilising the supply of power to the city.

TABLE 5A.6: Power Projection for Ganganagar

Year	t	t^2	y	log y	t log y
1975-76	–5	25	19.898	1.2988094	–6.494047
1976-77	–4	16	25.854	1.4125277	–5.650111
1977-78	–3	9	23.380	1.3688445	–4.106533
1978-79	–2	4	30.275	1.4810842	–2.962168
1979-80	–1	1	27.487	1.4391273	–1.439127
1980-81	0	0	24.946	1.3970009	0
1981-82	1	1	27.316	1.4364171	1.436417
1982-83	2	4	26.195	1.4182184	2.836436
1983-84	3	9	32.798	1.5158474	4.547542
1984-85	4	16	30.249	1.480711	5.922844
1985-86	5	25	33.991	1.5313639	7.656819
Total	11	110		15.779951	1.748072
1990-91	10	Y=AL 1.434541 + 0.0158915 × 10 = 39.215 mkWh			
1995-96	15	Y=AL 1.434541 + 0.0158915 × 15 = 47.088 mkWh			
2000-01	20	Y=AL 1.434541 + 0.0158915 × 20 = 56.542 mkWh			
2005-06	25	Y=AL 1.434541 + 0.0158915 × 25 = 67.984 mkWh			

Log Y = log a + log b.t

Log a = Σ log Y/N
= 15.779951/15
= 1.434541

Log b = Σ t *log* $Y/\Sigma t^2$
= 1.748072/110
= 0.0158915

Gr = (ALb-1)100
= (1.0372694-1)100
= 3.73%

Y = *AL* Log a + Log b.t
= *AL* 1.434541 + 0.0158915.t

5B. Power Profile of Jaipur City

Jaipur is not only the capital city of the State of Rajasthan for its administrative purpose, but a multifunctional city with industrial, commercial, educational and tourist establishments. A greater share of developed land of the city is occupied by residential houses followed by commercial, administrative, recreational uses and under streets and roads. As an example of the power utilization in a metropolitan town it needs an analytical evaluation of distribution of power to assess the power-consumption pattern for various functions of the city.

The city of Jaipur has a glorious history of its own. Probably the first planned city of India, the Old Walled City of Jaipur continues to enthral foreigners and fascinate Indians too. The name of the city at the time of its foundation (1727) was Sawai Jaipur on the name of the founder. Franclin called the town just "Jeypore". Tod also never used the title 'Sawai' while referring to "Jaipoor". The Roman spelling of the name of the city as "Jeypore" was first standardised in 1818 treaty with the British Government. From 1898 the modern spelling of 'Jaipur' was adopted for all official and unofficial purpose.

Growth of the City

The original town was confined to the city walls till the beginning of this century. It started growing outwards with the advent of railway line metalled roads and changing socio-economic factors. In the thirties Fatech Tiba, area south of Ramniwas Bagh, Ashok Nagar, New Colony in Jalupura and Bani Park residential schemes were conceived. Civil Lines area was developed primarily to house the senior Government servants. Two factors, firstly influx of displaced persons from Pakistan and secondly, being the capital of Rajasthan, were involved in the major growth of the city. After 1948 Congress Session at Jaipur, Bapunagar and Gandhinagar residential areas towards the south were developed. During the fifties when University of Rajasthan was established, the south-east area was also developed. Jhotwara Industrial area was developed in the early sixties with the extension towards north-west. With the establishment of Rajasthan Housing Board in 1970, two new housing colonies had come up at Jawahar Nagar in the east and Nahri-ka-Naka in the North-West, while another colony developed in Vanvihar. Moreover, new housing colonies for low-income group were set up near Ajmer Road, Station Road, Tonk Phatak and Galta Road. The growing residential areas made substantial increase in domestic power consumption of Jaipur.

Growth of Power Supply in Jaipur

The growth of power in the city of Jaipur can be traced back prior to Independence. Since the day of 18th November, 1727, when the foundations of the city was laid by the then Maharaja Swai Jai Singh II, the changing dimensions of development, socio-political and technological transformations have manifested manifold use of energy in its muscular and mechanical forms. For fifty years (1876-1926) the streets and many public buildings had been lit by gas under the rule of Late Maharaja Ram Singh, who wanted his city to beautify and modernise in many respects. The greater advantage of electricity which can supply both light and power, led to the question of building a Central Electricity Power House in Jaipur. Messers Vickers Petters a film of world wide repute was placed orders for semi-diesel engines of the total capacity of 650 kilowatt, two sets of 250 kW and one set of 150 kW capacity. The power house was situated near the Railway Station and had its own private siding for the supply of fuel direct from railway wagons into the power house storage tanks. In anticipation of demand of power for domestic, industrial and street lighting uses, distribution lines were erected and five transformer stations constructed. The Power House was formally opened by His Highness Maharaja Man Singh on 3rd January, 1927.

There was a considerable demand of power for domestic purposes and every prospect for industrial sector. A large number of oil engines were used for grinding corn which were a nuisance to neighbouring houses with their noise and noxious fumes. These engines were replaced by electric motors which were cheaper to buy and easier to operate. In addition to these mills, a good load was offered by the State Ginning Factory where a motor of 150 HP had been installed. This load was a most useful load to the power house since it was purely a day load. A number of public roads and buildings were lit with electricity and progress in this direction continued. The receipts of the department (Rs. 1,57,944) and the cost of working (Rs. 1,57,823)[2] were nearly equal during the year 1928-29. It was decided to close the Gas Works and street lighting had been replaced by electric illumination. The number of consumers of electricity continued to increase, raising the number and capacity of generating sets in the Power House. The number of sets, their capacity and year of installation is given in Table 5B.1.

Sources of Power Supply to Jaipur City

In addition to local power house, six transmission lines bring nearly one million kWh of power daily from Chambal System, Singrauli, Kota Thermal, RAPP and Bhakra System to the city of Jaipur.

(i) 132 kV Single Circuit Sawai Madhopur-Jaipur 140 km long transmission line was completed by the end of July 1962.
(ii) 132 kV Ratangarh-Jaipur emergency line was commenced on 7th December, 1964. This line was completed in a record time of 86

days to meet the power-shortage of the city due to reduction in power generation at Chambal from 9 lakh units to 5 lakh units per day.

(iii) 220 kV Hissar-Khetri-Jaipur Transmission line was completed in 1965-66.

(iv) 220 RAPP-Kota-Jaipur Double Circuit 234 km long transmission line was erected and energised in December 1972.

(v) 132 kV Bharatpur-Jaipur Single Circuit, 162 km long Transmission line was completed and energised on 11th November 1975.

(vi) 400 kV Extra-High-Tension transmission line from Chambal System is supplying power to Jaipur since December 1986. These High Tension and Extra High Tension transmission lines alongwith old Power House and Nallah Power House, make available nearly 42 thousand units of power per hour for the city.

TABLE 5B.1: Local Power Generating Sets of Jaipur

	Rated Capacity kW	Derated Capacity kW	Make	Year of installation
Diesel Generators:				
	1×500	1×300	Sulzer	—
	1×375	1×200	Sulzer	1927
	1×250	1×150	Sulzer	1931
	1×750	1×500	M.AN	1938
Total	1875	1150		
Turbo Sets:				
	2×2500	2×2300	Worthington	1951
	1×2500	1×1800	Worthington	1952
	1×3000	Out of Commission 2300	Doniel Admson	1957
Total	7500	6400		
G. total	9375	7550		

Source: Administrative Report RSEB, 1959.

H.T. Transmission Lines

The total length of 33 kV single circuit transmission line as on 31 March 1974 was 45 km and 33 kV Double circuit line was 55.5 km long in Jaipur. Whereas, 11 kV D/C line was spread in 22.92 km length and 11 kV S/C line was extended over 210.45 km to transmit power from Grid Sub Station and local Power Houses. The total length of H.T. lines in Jaipur city circle rose to 476.215 km at the end of March, 1980. The length of underground H.T. Transmission lines was only 59.584 km as against the over head H.T. lines of the order of 416.631 km. These transmission lines are classified with their length and nature of construction in the Table 5B.2.

TABLE 5B.2: **Transmission lines in Jaipur city circle**

Type	O.H./U.G.	km
33 kV.DC	O.H.	44.959
33 kV.SC	O.H.	48.150
11 kV.DC	O.H.	30.157
11 kV.SC	O.H.	293.365
11 kV.DC	U.G.	3.214
11 kV.SC	U.G.	56.370
Total		476.215

OH = Over Head,
UG = Underground
Source: Statistical Records of City Circle Jaipur, Circle Office, RSEB, Jaipur.

Distribution Lines

Power is distributed among its consumers through the distribution lines from the Step-down Sub Stations. These lines with an aggregate length of 1254.524 km at the end of March, 1980 comprised 6.6 kV lines (.41%), 3.3 kV lines (2.1%) and 420/230 kV lines (97.49%). There were 526 transformers with the installed capacity of 182,777 kVA at the end of fiscal year 1979-80. Segregation of these transformers is given in Table 5B.3.

Augmentation of Sub-Stations

The existing transmission and distribution system of Jaipur city is inadequate for meeting the present as well as anticipated load demand and for maintaining continuous stable supply. The load growth needs a

132 kV ring main and EHV Sub-Stations around the city. The power requirement is proposed to be met by pressing into service the new 33 kVDC. Ring main and Sub-Stations around Jaipur served from the existing 132 kV Chambal Grid Sub-Station, Dausa 132 kV GSS and Vishwakarma 132 kV GSS. In addition there should be provision for feeding this ring main from proposed 132/33 kV Sub-Station at Sanganer. The new 11 kV feeders should be laid and some others augmented.

TABLE 5B.3: Transformers installed in Jaipur

Type	Number	kVA Capacity
33/11 kV	14	66,500
11/3.3 kV	4	13,750
11/0.4 kV	461	91,882
6.6/0.4 kV	8	1,145
3.3/0.4 kV	38	7,625
3.3/6.6 kV	1	1,875
Total	526	1,82,777

Source: Statistical Reports of Jaipur City Circle 1980.

The augmentation of existing Durgapura Sub-Station from 1 mVA to 1×5 mVA has been proposed by the RSEB. Similarly, 1×5 mVA transformer has already been added at MR Engineering college Sub-Station in 1977. The transformation capacity of the existing sub-station at New Jhotwara and Old Jhotwara should be augmented. It is proposed to provide at least six bays to accommodate two incoming, two outgoing and two transformers. All the sub-stations should be inter-connected by the 33 kVDC Ring-Main with directional protections to facilitate the speedy elimination of the faulty section and maintain continuity of supply in the remaining healthy sections. The size of 33/11 kV transformers should be standardised and they should be adequately protected.

11 kV and LV Systems: To meet the growth of load and provide reliability in supply, it is necessary to establish new 33/11 kV Sub-Station on the periphery of the city. To feed the additional power to the consumers the 11 kV distribution network also requires additions and improvements. The development in the city are taking place at a tremendous speed as evident from the Master Plan and the activities of UIT, Housing Board, Rajasthan Industrial and Mineral Development

Corporation and other Government and private agencies. This justified the need of expanding the work of new sub-station and laying of new 11 kV LT lines to be able to satisfactorily meet the load growth.

Distribution system in some parts of the city is still served by obsolete 3.3 and 6.6 kV system which is not commercial and needs immediate changeover. Moreover, the system has outlived its useful life and can not be relied upon for continuity of supply. Therefore, the existing 33 kV and 6.6 kV feeders should be replaced by new 11 kV feeders. Similarly, the long used 3.3 kV and 6.6 kV switchgear and 33/ .4 and 6.6/ .4 kV transformers should be replaced with 11 kV switchgear and 11/ .4 kV transformers.

Consumers Growth Trends in Jaipur

Since the installation of local Power House in Jaipur in 1927, the number of consumers increased to 3500 in 1937. Due to increase in domestic, commercial, industrial and new water-supply connections the number of power consumers rose to 3769 at the end of March 1940 consuming nearly 30 lakhs of units of power. Data were not available for a long lapse of time but the number of consumers continued to increase which is evident by the growth trends revealed in Table 5B.4.

TABLE 5B.4: Consumers Growth Trends in Jaipur

Year	Consumers served	Annual variation	Per cent variation
1936-37	3,500	—	—
1937-38	3,514	14	0.50
1938-39	3,685	171	4.87
1939-40	3,769	84	2.28
1973-74	74,134	—	—
1974-75	80,146	6012	8.11
1975-76	87,326	7210	9.00
1976-77	94,781	7425	8.50
1977-78	102,894	8113	8.56
1978-79	112,258	9364	9.10
1979-80	121,569	9311	8.29
1980-81	131,981	10412	8.56
1981-82	143,111	11130	8.43
1982-83	152,301	9190	6.42
1983-84	158,553	6252	4.11
1984-85	165,368	6815	4.30
1985-86	181,767	16399	9.92
1986-87	192,172	10405	5.72

TABLE 5B.5: Sectoral growth trends of consumers (1974 87)

	Sector	No. of Consumers		Per cent of total		Per cent growth
		1973-74	1986-87	1973-74	1986-87	1974-87
I	Domestic	52,806	1,39,349	71.23	72.51	163.89
II	Commercial	17,561	45,351	23.67	23.60	158.25
III	Industrial	2,518	5,462	3.40	2.84	116.92
IV	Irrigation	1,044	917	1.41	0.48	(–)12.16
V	Street light	85	150	0.12	0.08	76.47
VI	Water supply	52	339	0.08	0.18	551.92
VII	Mix supply	68	604	0.09	0.31	788.24
	Total	74,134	1,92,172	100.00	100.00	159.22

Table 5B.5 reveals that the highest growth was registered by Mix Load consumers (788%) followed by water supply consumers (552%), Domestic consumers (163.89%), commercial (158%), industrial (117%) and street light (76.47%) during 1974-87. Irrigation consumers showed a decrease of 12.16 per cent during the thirteen years due to encroachment of residential colonies on agricultural land within municipal boundary of the city. Obviously, the number of domestic-consumers remained highest followed by commercial, industrial, irrigation, bulk, water supply and street-lighting consumers. More than 95 per cent connections were given to domestic and commercial consumers and rest of the five per cent to the remaining consumers of five sectors in the city.

Growth Trends of Power Consumption in Jaipur

Jaipur has made gigantic strides in the field of power utilization since the installation of generating sets in the city. The progress made in this sphere is fantastic if viewed in the light that Jaipur was the first city of Rajasthan to have its own Power House in thirties. During the year 1930-31, 11.6 lakhs of units were consumed in the city, which rose to 32.4 lakhs of units at the end of March 1943. Since then, the power scenario of Jaipur city have been fast changing. It is very significant to note that 7.84 per cent of the State's total power consumption in 1985-86 was utilised in Jaipur city. Moreover, 15.28 per cent power was shared by Jaipur in terms of urban power consumption in Rajasthan in the same year.

Growing industrialisation, increasing population and extending commercial activities, mainly have been responsible for the growth of power consumption in Jaipur. This is evident by the figures given in Table 5B.7 which shows that more than 80 per cent of power supplied to Jaipur, was consumed by industrial, domestic and commercial consumers. The domestic power consumption registered 420 per cent growth during 1974-87 followed by commercial (374.37%), mixed consumption (142%), water supply (124.73%), industrial (104%) and street lighting consumption (46.33%). Power consumption under irrigation decreased by 60.88 per cent during the period of thirteen years due to urban development.

TABLE 5B.6: Consumption Growth Trends (Consumption in mkWh)

Year	Consumption	Variation	% variation	% of State's total	% of State's urban consumption
1973-74	138.90	—	—	10.43	16.49
1974-75	154.62	15.72	11.32	9.88	16.12
1975-76	161.91	7.29	4.71	8.88	14.38
1976-77	182.07	20.16	12.45	8.64	14.30
1977-78	198.15	16.08	8.83	8.74	14.80
1978-79	216.63	18.48	9.33	7.95	14.15
1979-80	222.92	6.29	2.90	7.51	14.79
1980-81	211.083	11.837	5.31	7.21	15.03
1981-82	224.572	13.489	6.39	7.17	14.92
1982-83	236.310	11.738	5.23	7.23	15.85
1983-84	300.789	64.479	27.29	7.25	14.64
1984-85	344.444	43.655	14.51	7.85	15.04
1985-86	377.000	32.556	9.45	7.84	15.28
1986-87	388.612	11.612	3.08	—	—

TABLE 5B.7: Sectoral Growth Trends of Power Consumption

Sector	Million kWh		Per cent of total		Per cent growth
	1973-74	1986-87	1973-74	1986-87	1974-87
I Industrial	77.08	157.137	55.49	40.44	103.86
II Domestic	20.81	108.193	14.98	27.84	419.91
III Commercial	15.00	71.156	10.80	18.31	374.37
IV Water Supply	14.87	33.418	10.71	8.60	124.73
V Street light	1.88	2.751	1.35	0.71	46.33
VI Irrigation	3.18	1.244	2.29	0.32	–60.88
VII Mixed	6.08	14.713	4.38	3.78	141.99
Total	138.90	388.612	100.00	100.00	179.78

Spatial Pattern of Power and its Consumers in Jaipur

Nine Zones, demarcated by the RSEB for their administrative purpose, have been taken into consideration to assess the spatial pattern of distribution of power in Jaipur. Zone-wise distribution of consumers as well as power consumption is given in Table 5B.8.

It is interesting to note that the highest number of consumers in A II Zone sharing nearly 13.7 per cent of total, consumed only 5.89 per cent of total power consumption. Whereas, C I Zone sharing only 11.38 per cent consumers of the city consumed 30.46 per cent of total power utilised in 1980 due to concentration of large scale industries. More detail picture of power distribution illustrated by Fig. 5B.1.

Observation

The maximum demand around the year 1961 was of the order of 9 mW only, which has been registering tremendous growth since then. The then existing 3.3 kV sub-transmission system was not found satisfactory, therefore, 11 kV sub-transmission was erected around the city. The peak demand continued to increase. It was 75 mW in 1978, 97 mW in 1980, 115 mW in 1982 and 136 mW in 1985. Hence, the 11 kV sub-transmission system is again being replaced by 33 kV sub-transmission ring-main system so as to meet the increasing load of power.

TABLE 5B.8: Distribution of Consumers and Consumption of Power in Jaipur City, 1980

Zone		No. of consumers	% of the total	Consumption in mkWh	% of the total
A	I	13,644	11.23	24.62	11.04
	II	16,632	13.68	13.14	5.89
	III	10,424	8.57	9.36	4.20
B	I	14,545	11.96	18.64	8.36
	II	13,429	11.05	28.15	12.64
	III	12,270	10.09	19.51	8.75
C	I	13,844	11.38	67.90	30.46
	II	11,746	9.66	8.23	3.69
	III	15,035	12.38	33.37	14.97
Total		121,569	100.00	222.92	100.00

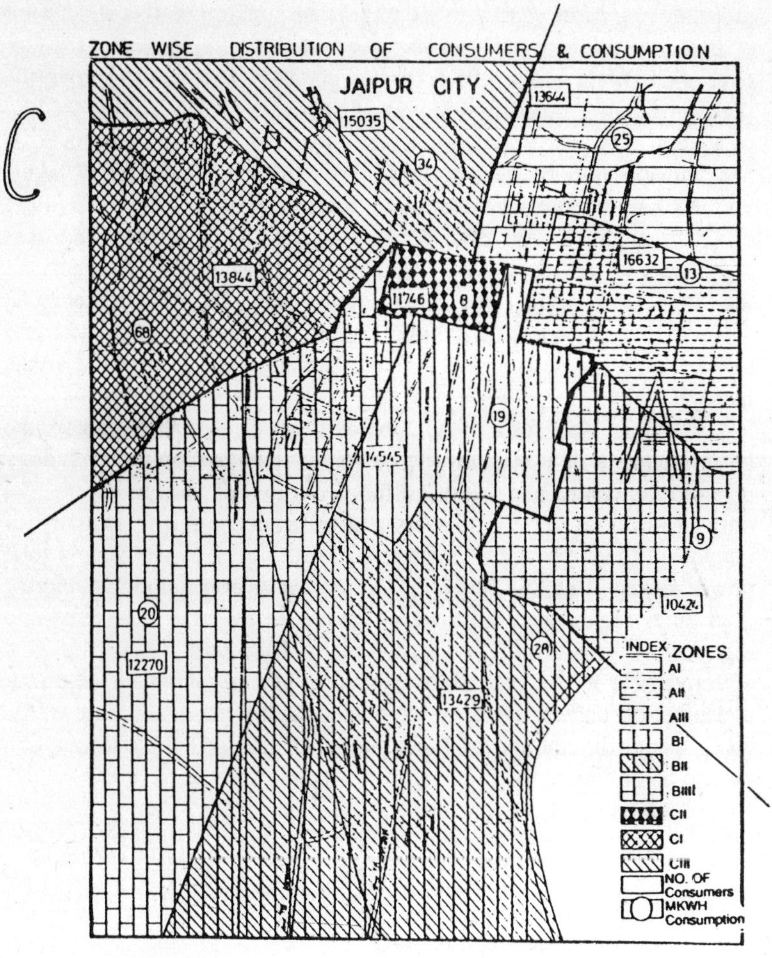
ZONE WISE DISTRIBUTION OF CONSUMERS & CONSUMPTION
JAIPUR CITY
15035
34
13644
25
16632
13
11746
8
13844
68
19
14545
9
10424
20
12270
13429
INDEX ZONES
AI
AII
AIII
BI
BII
BIII
CII
CI
CIII
NO. OF Consumers
MKWH Consumption

FIG. 5B.1

The city of Jaipur extends over an area of about 206 square km and growing year after year with its increasing population as well as their economic activities. The population increased by 52.5 per cent in 1971 over 1961, when it was 4.03 lakhs. As per 1971 Census (6.15 lakh) the per capita power consumption was of the order of 225 kWh at the end of March 1974. The population again registered an increase of 58.8 per cent in 1981 over the Census 1971. As per 1981 Census (9.77 lakhs) the per capita power consumption increased by 4 kWh over 1971 Census reaching to 230 kWh per head at the end of March 1982. It is significant to contrast the per capita power consumption of Jaipur and the State as a whole. The State average was 48 kWh per head in 1973-74, 4.7 times less than that of Jaipur. The State average increased to 90.3 kWh per head in 1981-82 remaining only 2.55 times less than its capital city.

Consumer type, form of function and pattern of distribution are the basic elements of Power Profile of Jaipur. Power-supply-morphology of an urban centre like Jaipur, differs from that of the rural sector not only in terms of variety of users and utilization but also in terms of connected load. The city consumed 7.84 per cent of the State's total power during 1985-86. Similarly, the per capita consumption exhibited 2.55 times higher than the State's average 90 kWh per head. The city registered a growth of 171.42 per cent in 1986 over 1974. The most effective role in the process of evolution and development of power consumption pattern seems to have been multifunctional nature of the city. Spatial distribution of functions have provided the consumption pattern an outline or the frame within which the whole picture is set.

NOTES

1. Gr = (1.0060763-1) 100 = 0.61%
2. Administrative Reports of Jaipur, 1929.

6

ENERGY DIFFERENTIATION PATTERN IN RAJASTHAN

ENERGY DIFFERENTIATIONS take many forms. It differs from region to region and sector to sector. Fishermen in a poor island communities such as the Lakshadweep may have shortage of oil to operate their boats and farmers in the main land of India to work their irrigation pumps. The energy crisis for domestic sector means the shortage of fire-wood and for industrial sector it means the shortage of coal or electricity. The use of energy in the world is grossly imbalanced. All the fuel used by the third World for all purposes is only slightly more than the amount of gasoline the Developed World burns to move its automobiles.

The objective of the present study is to examine the inter-district and inter-sector variations in the consumption pattern of electricity in Rajasthan both at the district and sector levels. For this purpose the sectoral energy consumption variations, areal energy variations, per capita and per square kilometre energy variations and the variations in rural electrification have also been taken into consideration. Income and expenditure on power have been taken into account so as to reckon the cost-benefit of power industry of the State.

6A. Sectoral Patterns of Power Distribution

The energy problem of a given region cannot be properly examined without the evaluation of its sectoral distribution pattern. With the completion of plans and modernisation of industrial, agricultural and other economic activities, the pattern of sectoral differentiation of power changes. Table 6A.1 gives the energy demand patterns among different sectors in India.

TABLE 6A.1: Sectoral Differentiation Pattern of Power in India (Percentage of Total Power Consumption)

Sectors	1951	1960-61	1970-71	1980-81	1981-82	1982-83	1983-84	1984-85
Industrial	63.8	69.4	67.6	58.4	58.8	55.9	56.7	55.6
Domestic	12.4	10.7	8.8	11.2	11.5	12.5	12.9	13.3
Agriculture	4.2	6.0	10.2	17.6	16.8	18.5	17.7	18.7
Commercial	6.9	6.1	5.9	5.7	6.0	6.3	5.9	6.1
Traction	6.9	3.3	3.2	2.7	2.8	2.7	2.6	2.5
Others	5.9	4.5	4.3	4.4	4.1	4.1	4.1	3.8

Source:1. Central Electricity Authority: Public Electricity Supply— All India Statistics, 1970-81.
2. *Economic Survey*, 1985-86.

The above table shows that during the period 1951-85, there was a rapid increase of power demand in agricultural sector with a reduction in industrial sector. The other sectors show marginal changes. Domestic and commercial sectors are static, while traction and other sectors exhibit declining trend.

District-wise sectoral distribution of consumers of power in Rajasthan (Fig. 6.1) computed in per cent of total, reveals that 12-16 districts remained below the State's average and 7-11 districts above the average. Figure 6.2 shows that 15-17 districts consumed below the State's average and 6-8 district above the State's average power consumption in 1980. The trend of sectoral power distribution was more or less the same in 1985 (Fig. 6.3). Rajasthan is one such State in India where a lot of differentiations in sectoral power consumption are found because of the unbalanced development of economic activities. Like the Indian union, agricultural sector is one of the most important sectors in the economy of the State which contributes 44.52 per cent of State's total domestic product, employing 72 per cent of the State's labour force, and consuming 32 per cent electric power of the State's total energy consumption. The sectoral energy differentiation pattern in Rajasthan from the percentage of total power consumption point of view reveals the following picture, illustrated in Table 6A.2.

The pattern of power utilization in Rajasthan since the year 1959-60 to 1980-81 exhibited an increasing trend of percentage of power-consumption under the agricultural sector, and then a slight fluctuation in the following years. Whereas the industrial sector tended to reduce its share of the total power consumption. Agricultural sector

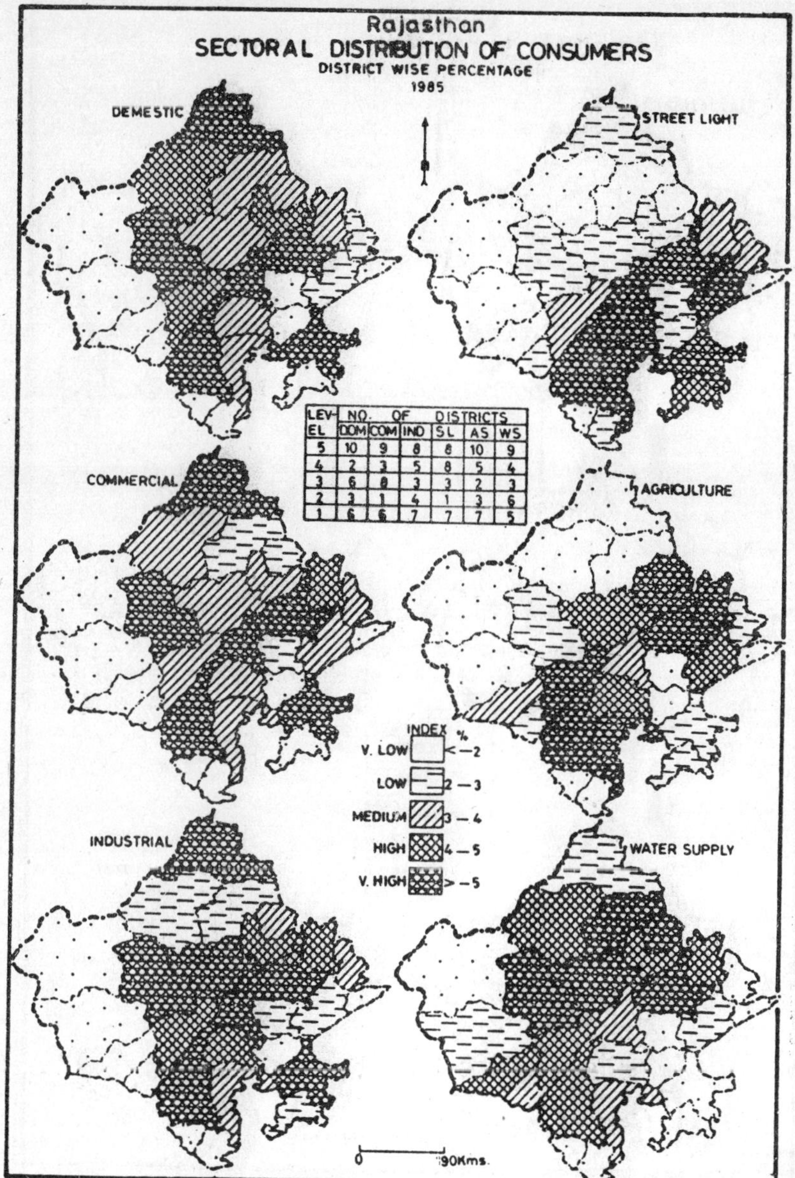

LEVEL	NO. OF DISTRICTS					
	DOM	COM	IND	SL	AS	WS
5	10	9	8	8	10	9
4	2	3	5	8	5	4
3	6	8	3	3	2	3
2	3	1	4	1	3	6
1	6	6	7	7	7	5

FIG. 6.1

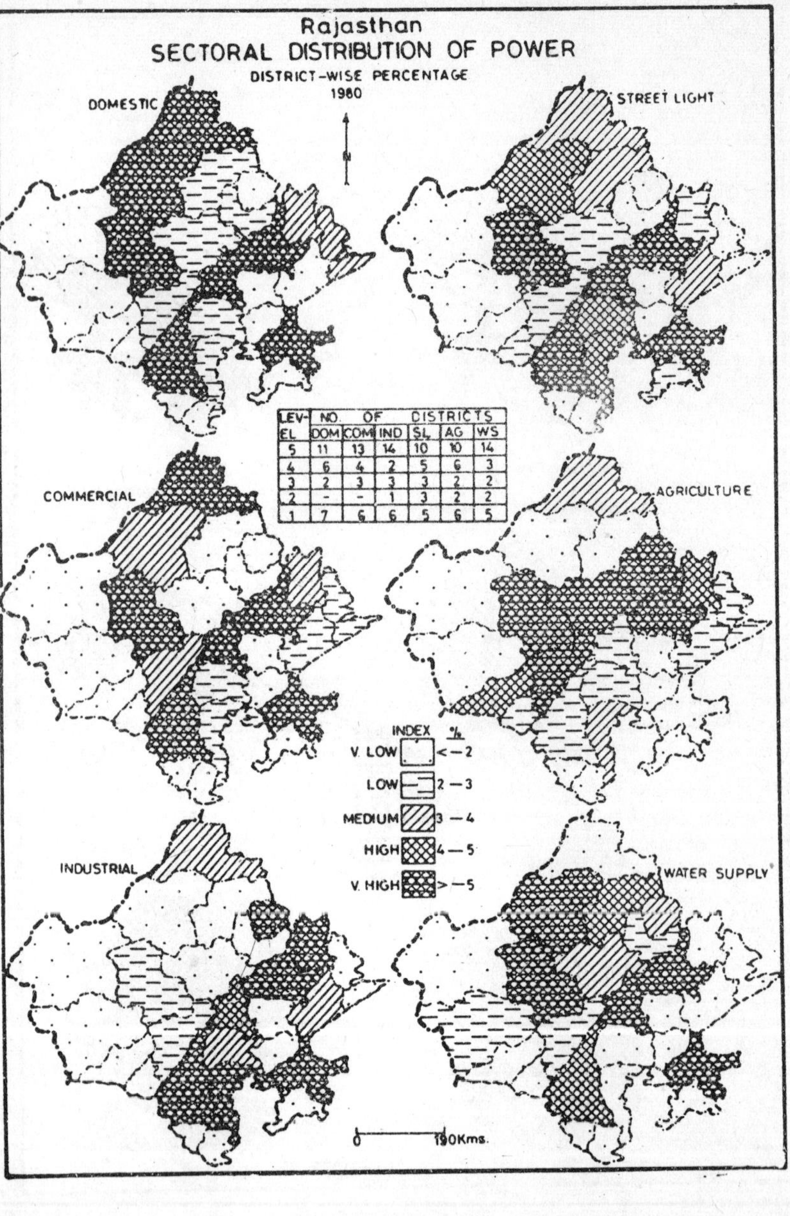

LEVEL	NO. OF DISTRICTS					
	DOM	COM	IND	SL	AG	WS
5	11	13	14	10	10	14
4	6	4	2	5	6	3
3	2	3	3	3	2	2
2	-	-	1	3	2	2
1	7	6	6	5	6	5

FIG. 6.2

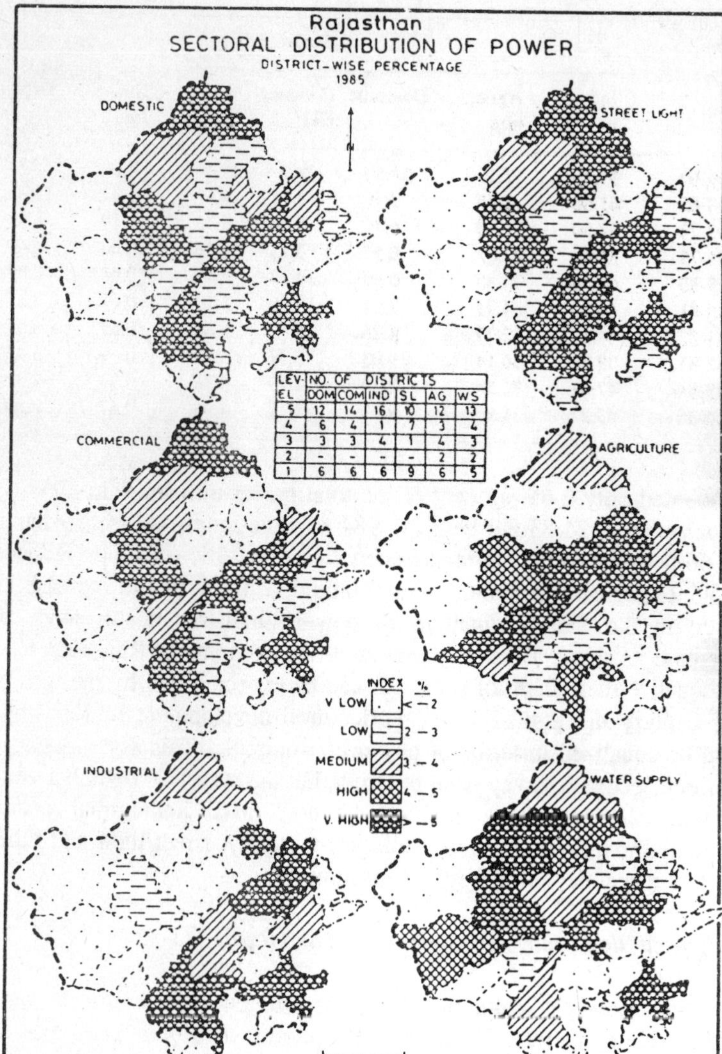

LEVEL	NO. OF DISTRICTS					
	DOM	COM	IND	SL	AG	WS
5	12	14	16	10	12	13
4	6	4	1	7	3	4
3	3	3	4	1	4	3
2	-	-	-	-	2	2
1	6	6	6	9	6	5

FIG. 6.3

TABLE 6A.2: Sectoral Differentiation Pattern of Power in Rajasthan (Percentage of Total Power Consumption)

Year	Sector						
	Indust-rial	Agricul-ture	Domestic	Commer-cial	Water Supply	Street light	Others
1959-60	33.20	7.10	21.50	18.9	23.40	4.00	-
1964-65	61.66	2.65	7.35	7.11	6.19	1.82	13.22
1969-70	59.50	11.40	6.70	5.80	6.70	1.10	8.88
1974-75	55.61	22.07	6.57	5.13	5.36	0.80	4.49
1979-80	49.54	30.85	6.88	4.72	4.49	0.68	2.84
1980-81	44.20	34.31	7.57	4.90	5.10	0.67	3.25
1981-82	44.63	32.77	8.26	5.17	5.04	0.58	3.55
1982-83	39.79	36.14	9.03	5.71	5.22	0.69	3.42
1983-84	47.93	31.34	8.20	4.73	4.36	0.59	2.82
1984-85	45.23	31.83	9.23	5.17	4.98	0.67	2.89

accounted only 2.65 per cent of the total power utilization in 1964-65 which rose to 31.83 per cent in 1984-85. The industrial sector shared 61.66 per cent of the aggregate energy used in 1964-65 which reduced to 45.23 per cent in 1984-85. Agricultural sector seems to increase its share in the State's quantum of power. Industrial sector tends to decrease its share. These two sectors of the economy of Rajasthan tend to equalize their share of power. It can be expected that by the turn of the century the industrial and agricultural development in Rajasthan will be equalized in terms of power consumption. This assumption, at present, seems far away from the truth, but the statistics looks like that. Among the remaining sectors domestic and commercial sector exhibited marginal changes, while water supply, street light and other sectors reveal declining trend of consumption.

Differentiation Pattern between Urban and Rural Sectors

An urban power consumption pattern is different than that of the rural consumption pattern in terms of sectoral distribution of power. Agricultural sector is predominant above all other sectors in rural areas. In an urban centre the industrial sector is prime consumer of power. It is interesting to note that 80 per cent population living in 35 thousand villages is still consuming less than 50 per cent of the total power available in Rajasthan. On the other hand rest of the 20 per cent urban population living in two hundred towns and cities consumes more than 50 per cent of the State's power. The degree of differentiation between rural and urban sectors was much higher during the previous decade. In the year 1970-71, 80 per cent population (rural) consumed less than 25 per cent quantum of power and 20 per cent population (urban) consumed more than 75 per cent power of the State. It is encouraging to note that the differentiation of power distribution between urban and rural sectors have been decreasing. By the coming year the rural sector will have to have 50 per cent share of power. The quantum of power should be in proportion of the size of area and population so as to fasten the rate of economic development. Table 6A.3 shows the changing distributional pattern of power consumption in urban and rural sectors in Rajasthan.

TABLE 6A.3: Segregation of Distribution of Power between Urban and Rural Sectors in Rajasthan

Year	Urban Sector		Rural Sector		Aggregate mkWh
	mkWh	%	mkWh	%	
1970-71	728.69	75.99	230.23	24.01	958.92
1971-72	802.12	72.63	302.34	27.37	1104.46
1972-73	853.53	67.66	408.05	32.34	1261.58
1973-74	842.05	63.24	489.41	36.76	1331.41
1974-75	959.02	61.30	605.39	38.70	1564.41
1975-76	1126.22	61.79	696.44	38.21	1822.41
1976-77	1272.96	60.40	834.44	39.60	2107.40
1977-78	1339.09	59.04	928.89	40.96	2267.98
1978-79	1531.26	56.20	1193.56	43.80	2724.82
1979-80	1506.84	50.75	1462.15	49.25	2968.99
1980-81	1404.86	47.96	1524.10	52.04	2928.96
1981-82	1505.45	48.08	1625.95	51.92	3131.40
1982-83	1490.70	45.60	1778.09	54.40	3268.79
1983-84	2055.24	49.54	2093.47	50.46	4148.71
1984-85	2290.09	52.21	2096.47	47.79	4386.56
1985-86	2467.97	51.33	2340.05	48.67	4808.02

Source: Annual Reports of RSEB from 1971 to 1986.

Power differentiation trends are exhibited here in the form of total power utilized in urban and rural areas under agricultural and industrial sectors (Table 6A.4). The industrial sector shows decreasing trend both in urban and rural areas. Whereas on the other side the agricultural sector shows marginal change in urban areas and gradually increasing trend in rural areas. Since 1980, the agriculture in rural sector and industries in urban sector tend to equalize their share in their respective areas. As in the year 1984-85, 59.6 per cent of rural power was used in agriculture and 59.2 per cent of urban power was consumed in industrial sectors.

TABLE 6A.4: Segregation of Energy Distribution Between Agriculture and Industrial Sectors (in percentage of the total Urban and Rural Power Consumption)

Year	Agriculture Sector		Industrial Sector	
	Urban	Rural	Urban	Rural
1970-71	3.09	38.69	66.45	51.09
1971-72	4.34	39.31	67.26	51.94
1972-73	4.46	46.71	66.93	44.36
1973-74	5.05	48.46	64.79	42.89
1974-75	4.51	49.91	64.56	41.44
1975-76	3.76	44.65	68.56	45.84
1976-77	3.63	45.98	67.96	44.84
1977-78	3.42	43.35	67.61	46.48
1978-79	3.87	48.30	68.14	43.03
1979-80	5.35	57.13	63.77	34.88
1980-81	4.79	61.52	59.69	29.92
1981-82	6.09	57.47	57.87	32.37
1982-83	6.04	61.38	53.04	28.68
1983-84	4.75	57.51	62.74	33.38
1984-85	6.40	59.60	59.20	29.96
1985-86	4.27	57.62	60.06	31.02

The industrial and agricultural sectors utilized 40 per cent of State's total power in 1959-60 which rose to 77 per cent in 1984-85. The changes in agricultural sector or the industrial sector of a region can largely be understood through changes in sectoral power consumption for the analysis of which it is necessary to identify the areas of low and high power consumption. Such an analysis would cast light on the rate of growth of a particular region compared to the other region. Further for any policy recommendation it is necessary to assess the causes of high and low rate of growth.

6B. Areal Differentiation Pattern of Power

Areal differentiation of energy system is a function of production, consumption and exchange of power over time and space. Demand generated by individuals, groups or society as a whole for energy requirement like a wide range of goods and services, is the force that motivates the function. Business organisations and institutional organs emerge to meet the demand. Supply takes place. Distances differ between points of demand and generation of power which effects the degree and mode of supply. Demand and supply of power aptly regulate the process of economic development which have an areal complexion. Areal differentiation comes into being with the emergence of an economic system. Place and people, policy and production, and the price and pace of development determine the degree of differentiation.

Energy resources like other natural resources have never been equally distributed neither by nature nor by the man himself. Rajasthan is one of such States in India where a lot of areal differentiation in power-distribution is found. The district level differentiation of power has been taken into consideration so as to calculate the disparity in power consumption pattern in Rajasthan.

Obviously, the quantum of power utilized in Rajasthan is lower in the entire State and there exist a large differentiation between lower and higher district consumer. To assess the level of differentiation of power-distribution in Rajasthan at district level six variables have been taken into account. These variables are: (i) number of consumers, (ii) power consumed in millions of units, (iii) capacity of transformers in kVA, (iv) number of villages electrified, (v) number of Harijan Basties electrified, and (vi) number of wells energised (Appendix Table 6B.1). District-wise percentage of the State's total, separately for each of the variables, have been worked out (Appendix Table 6B.2). The State has been regionalised in five regions on the basis of percentage of a variable under a district. The analysis exhibits the fact that higher the percentage of a variable, lower the level of differentiation, and lower the percentage of the variable higher the level of differentiation. The districts have been categorised into five such levels, two below the State's average and two above the average. The districts have been arranged in a tabular form given on next page. The results are illustrated in Fig. 6B.1.

6C. Per Capita Power Consumption

Per capita consumption of electricity is an accepted and proven standard by which a State can be judged of its economic development. In view of the fact that the per capita consumption of electricity in Rajasthan is very low, its future consumption is very likely to go up. Table 6C.1 shows the growth of per capita consumption of electricity in Rajasthan in comparison to national per capita power consumption.

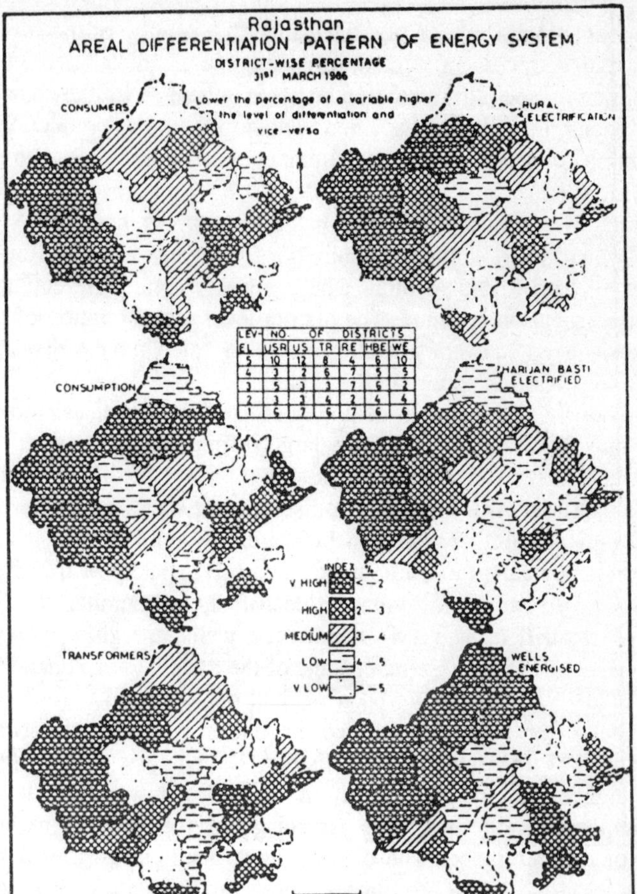
Rajasthan
AREAL DIFFERENTIATION PATTERN OF ENERGY SYSTEM
DISTRICT-WISE PERCENTAGE
31ST MARCH 1986
Lower the percentage of a variable higher the level of differentiation and vice-versa
CONSUMERS
RURAL ELECTRIFICATION
CONSUMPTION
HARIJAN BASTI ELECTRIFIED
TRANSFORMERS
WELLS ENERGISED
LEVEL | NO. OF DISTRICTS: USR US TR RE HBE WE
5 | 10 12 8 4 6 10
4 | 3 2 6 7 5 5
3 | 5 3 3 7 6 2
2 | 3 3 4 2 4 4
1 | 5 7 6 7 6 6
INDEX
V HIGH < 2
HIGH 2 – 3
MEDIUM 3 – 4
LOW 4 – 5
V LOW > 5
0 100Kms

FIG. 6B.1

Tabulation of Areal Differentiation Pattern of Energy System

Variables	Below the average		Average 3-4%	Above the average	
	< 2% V. High	2-3% High	Medium	4-5% Low	> 5% V. Low
1	2	3	4	5	6
Consumers Benefited	Banswara Barmer, Bundi, Dholpur, Dungarpur, Jalore, Jhalawar, Jaisalmer Sirohi, Tonk (10)	Bharatpur Churu Sawai -Madhopur (3)	Bhilwara, Bikaner Chittor-garh Jhun-jhunu Nagor (5)	Alwar Pali Sikar (3)	Ajmer Jaipur Jodhpur Kota Ganganagar Udaipur (6)
Consumption of Power	Banswara, Barmer, Bikaner, Dholpur, Dungarpur Jaisalmer Bharatpur, Bundi, Churu, Jalore, Jhalawar Tonk (12)	Sawai-Madhopur Sirohi (2)	Bhilwara Nagor Pali (3)	Chittor-garh, Jodh-pur Sri Ganganagar (3)	Ajmer, Alwar, Jaipur, Kota Jhunjhunu, Sikar, Udaipur (7)
Transformer kVA Capacity	Banswara Barmer, Bikaner, Dholpur, Dungarpur Jaisalmer Sirohi, Tonk (8)	Bundi Jalore Jhunjhunu Jhalawar Pali Sawai-Madhopur (6)	Bharatpur Churu Ganganagar (3)	Ajmer Bhilwara Chittorgarh Nagor (4)	Alwar, Jaipur Jodhpur, Kota Sikar, Udaipur (6)
Villages Electrified	Barmer, Bikaner Dholpur Jaisalmer (4)	Bundi, Churu Dungarpur Jalore, Jodh-pur, Sirohi Tonk (7)	Ajmer, Banswara Bharatpur, Jhalawar, Jhunjhunu, Pali, Sikar (7)	Nagor, Sawai-Madhopur (2)	Alwar, Bhil-wara, Chittor-garh, Jaipur, Kota, Ganga-nagar, Udaipur (7)

(Contd.)

1	2	3	4	5	6
Harijan Basties Electrified	Banswara, Barmer, Bundi, Dholpur, Dungarpur, Jaisalmer (6)	Alwar, Bikaner, Churu, Jodhpur, Sirohi (5)	Bharatpur, Jhanjhunu, Jalore, Kota Nagor, Tonk (6)	Ajmer, Sawai-Sikar Sri Ganga-nagar (4)	Bhilwara Chittorgarh, Jaipur, Pali, Jhalawar, Udaipur (6)
Wells Energised	Banswara, Barmer, Bikaner, Bundi, Churu, Dholpur, Dungarpur, Jaisalmer, Sriganga-nagar, Tonk (10)	Bharatpur, Jhalawar, Jodhpur, Kota, Sirohi (5)	Ajmer, Jalore (2)	Bhilwara, Nagor, Pali, Sawai-Madhopur (4)	Alwar, Chittor-garh, Jaipur, Jhunjhunu, Sikar, Udaipur (6)

TABLE 6C.1: Per Capit Power Consumption (in kWh)

	Year								
	1950-51	1960-61	1970-71	1980-81	1981-82	1982-83	1983-84	1984-85	1985-86
India	18	38	90	132	141	146	156		
Rajasthan	3	12	37.2	90.1	90.3	91.3	114.7	118.6	124.0

Above table reveals that the per capita consumption of power in the country in 1960-61 was only 38 kWh which rose to 156 kWh in 1983-84 whereas in Rajasthan it was 12 kWh, more than 3 times below the national average in 1960-61 which rose to 114.7 kWh in 1983-84. The State exhibited below the all-India average since the very beginning. The per capita consumption of electricity is very low in Assam, Himachal Pradesh, Jammu and Kashmir alike Rajasthan as they are a little behind the other States in the development of power sector. It is anticipated that this will be rectified in the coming years in these States.

The per capita use of power in the world is grossly unbalanced. The consumption of energy per head in industrialised countries compared to middle-income and low-income countries is in the proportion of 100 : 10 : 1. One American uses as much commercial energy as two Germans or Australian, three Swiss or Japanese, six Yugoslavs, nine Mexicans or Cubans, 16 Chinese, 19 Malaysians, 53 Indian or Indonesians, 109 Sri Lankans, 438 Malians, or 1072 Nepalese.* India is far behind than the developed countries in terms of per capita power consumption. The authorities have to increase it 18 times of the present level to equal the per capita level of Japan and 26 times to achieve the level of Australia or Germany. In view of the continuous depletion of the existing resources of energy and the continuous growth of population, the per head consumption of power in India though increased considerably to 156 kWh in 1983 compared to 18 kWh in 1950, is still 35 times and 53 times lower than that of U.K. and U.S.A. respectively.

The per capita consumption of electricity in Rajasthan is below the national average, as a whole. However several districts have exhibited their level above the national average. The following table shows the levels of per capita consumption of electricity for all the districts during the year 1984-85.

TABLE 6C.2: Levels of per Capita Power Consumption

Level	Per Capita Use in kWh	No.of Districts	Name of Districts
V	< 50	7	Banswara, Barmer, Churu, Dholpur, Dungarpur, Jaisalmer, Tonk.
IV	50- 100	9	Ganganagar, S. Madhopur, Nagor, Jhalawar, Jalore, Bundi, Bikaner, Bhilwara, Bharatpur
III	100- 150	5	Ajmer, Chittorgarh, Jodhpur, Pali, Sikar
II	150- 200	5	Alwar, Jaipur, Jhunjhunu, Sirohi, Udaipur
I	> 200	1	Kota.

The per capita power consumption is above the national average (156 kWh) in six districts namely, Kota, (296 kWh), Jhunjhunu

* North-South: A Programme for Survival, Pan Books London 1980, pp. 160-171.

(199.4 kWh), Jaipur (197.6 kWh), Alwar (176.9 kWh), Udaipur (170.5 kWh) and Sirohi (164.7 kWh). Rest of the 21 districts remained below the national average which is an indicator of the economic underdevelopment and low level of living standard (Fig. 6B.1).

Table 6C.3 depicts that in urban areas per capita power consumption increased broadly two-fold during 1971-86, while in the rural areas during the same period it registered almost eight-fold increase. It can be emphasised here that the rural electrification has been considered a matter of greater significance by the authorities. This is evident with the fact that where in 1971, the per capita urban power consumption was 18 times higher than that of the rural sector, remained only 3.8 times higher in 1986 due to rapidly increasing rural electrification.

TABLE 6C.3: Variation in Per Capita Power Consumption in Urban and Rural Sectors (in kWh)

Year	Per Capita Power Consumption		
	Urban	Rural	Rajasthan
1971	160.36	8.49	37.21
1981	194.82	56.34	90.08
1982	205.41	58.71	90.34
1983	197.99	62.71	91.32
1984	263.66	72.12	114.67
1985	283.85	70.55	118.64
1986	295.64	76.94	124.00

6D. Rural Electrification

Energy problem of Rajasthan should be studied in the context of 79 per cent of its population living in 34,968 inhabited villages. The rural population is expected to grow from 2,71,22 thousand in 1981 to 4,49,30 thousand in 2001. The bulk of this population will be engaged in agricultural activities hence we should concentrate our attention largely on meeting the energy needs of the rural sector of the area under study.

Rural electrification is a powerful tool for the economic development and social transformation of Rajasthan. Green revolution in the country, has attracted much attention in implementing the schemes of rural electrification. It is recognised that the laws of economics on the one hand and practical politics on the other have tended to influence very strongly the pattern and pace of electrification. Several times economic issues are encashed by ruling politicians on the one hand and certain problems are made political slogans by the opposition. The drought situation is being exploited and the problem of unemployment is made a slogan of political game. Creation of job opportunities in the rural areas by establishing small scale, subsidiary and cottage industries merely can be made possible by the adequate and stable supply of electrical energy to the rural areas, whether from conventional or from non-conventional sources.

Growth or Rural Electrification

As a matter of fact, rural electrification is a powerful agent of rural rehabilitation. The supply of power remained confined only to large cities of the princely States of Rajputana. At the time of the formation of Rajasthan only 42 rural localities had been electrified. The proportion consumed by rural electrification accounted for barely about one per cent of the total power consumption of the State.

During the First Five Year Plan 24 localities were added increasing the number of electrified villages to 66. In the early years population size of villages constituted the main basis for the selection of rural electrification. The green revolution shifted the emphasis from population size to potentiality of increasing the agricultural production. During the Second Five Year Plan the number of electrified rural localities increased by 65 and nearly doubled the figure of First Plan from 66 to 131. At the end of Third Five Year Plan rural electrification registered a tremendous rate of growth achieving the figure of 1242 villages being electrified. Rural electrification made a gradual increase achieving 17.6 per cent, 30.4 per cent and 56.9 per cent at the year ending Fourth, Fifth and Sixth Five Year Plans respectively.

Rajasthan State Electricity Board has taken keen interest in the programmes of rural electrification. It has subsidised the programmes of rural electrification by keeping the rates of tariff low, levying electricity surcharges at the lower rates of ten per cent in place of fifteen per cent and forgiving completely the electricity duty. During 1964 to 1967 the State was in the grip of severe power shortage due to failure of rains. Consequently, 35 to 60 per cent power cuts were imposed and new connections were restricted. In spite of such a severe natural calamity the programmes of rural electrification were not made to suffer, neither power cuts were imposed, nor restrictions were placed on new connections. Hence, 62.7 per cent census villages have been electrified so far benefiting 73.82 per cent of State's population. Limited funds, rising prices of materials like copper and steel, and prohibitive cost of transmission of electricity to the far flung areas have held back the programmes of rural electrification. Details of progress of rural electrification in Rajasthan is given in the Table 6D.1 and illustrated in Fig. 6D.3.

TABLE 6D.1: Plan-wise Progress of Rural Electrification

Plan	Rajasthan		India	
	Localities electrified	Percentage electrification	Localities electrified	Percentage electrification
At the time of formation of Rajasthan	42	0.10	3061	0.5
First five year plan	66	0.20	7294	1.3
Second five year plan	131	0.40	21750	3.8
Third five year plan	1242	3.85	45144	7.8
Three annual plans	2160	6.54	73732	12.8
Fourth five year plan	5892	17.61	156729	27.2
Fifth five year plan	10156	30.35	216863	37.6
Two annual plans	13988	41.80	249799	43.4
Sixth five year plan	20444	56.87	360792	62.7

Source: Annual Reports of RSEB & Reports of Energy, Deptt. Govt. of India.

Observation

The rural electrification programme has got much impetus. At the end of 1968-69, the proportion of energy consumed in rural electrification to total power consumed in the State had reached 10 per cent which was accounted for barely 1.0 per cent at the time of the formation of Rajasthan.

In 1951 there were only 42 electrified localities consisting 26 towns and 16 villages. Power supply was then confined to only domestic, street and commercial lighting. The rural electrification received low priority in fifties and sixties. The pace of rural electrification picked up in the decade 1969-79. During the Fifth Five Year Plan 10,156 villages were electrified, raising the level of village electrification to 30.35 per cent.

The impressive result was a fivefold increase in the rural electrification and about ninefold increase in pumpsets energisation over the previous decade. Sustained efforts in rural electrification have led to another 10,288 villages being electrified raising the number to 20,444 during 1979-85. Rural electrification has thus risen to 56.87 per cent and the total number of agriculture wells energised to 2,74,169.

It is estimated that the level of rural electrification by the March 1988 is likely to rise 65.99 per cent. But it is a matter of investigation (i) that how much houses were actually electrified in an electrified village, (ii) that how long the electric current in full swing is available. People do not tend to have domestic connections and power supply do tend to fluctuate. Thus the situation is balanced and authorities are proud of increasing the percentage of rural electrification on papers.

It seems essential to be identified that how many rural houses are benefited by increasing number of village electrification. Having sufficient facilities for supply of electricity to individual household, less than 15 per cent houses have their connections. Several politico-socio-economic factors influence the actual percentage of rural electrification. For instance (i) people still believing in the use of traditional sources of house lighting and they do not want to take electric connection, (ii) some of them want it but their low purchasing power inhibits them to do so. Here the obvious situation is of struggle between consumers will-power and purchasing power, (iii) there is another group of people able to purchase but they do not have power connection due to institutional malpractices. In the last case, political and institutional powers are controlling factors. Figures 6D.1 and 6D.2 illustrate the interaction between power components in the management of power distribution. The model is a matter of further investigation conducting micro-areal studies.

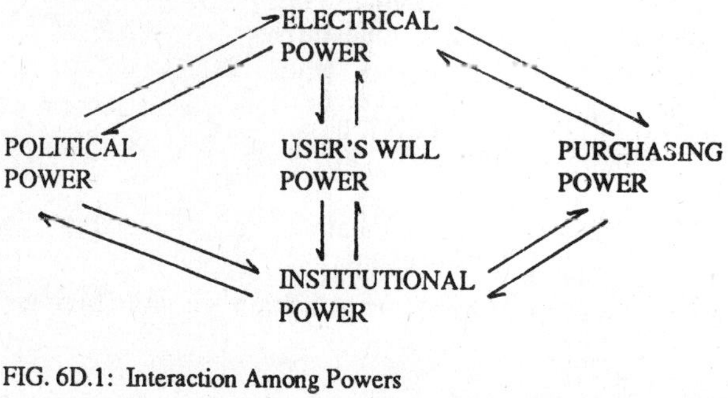

FIG. 6D.1: Interaction Among Powers

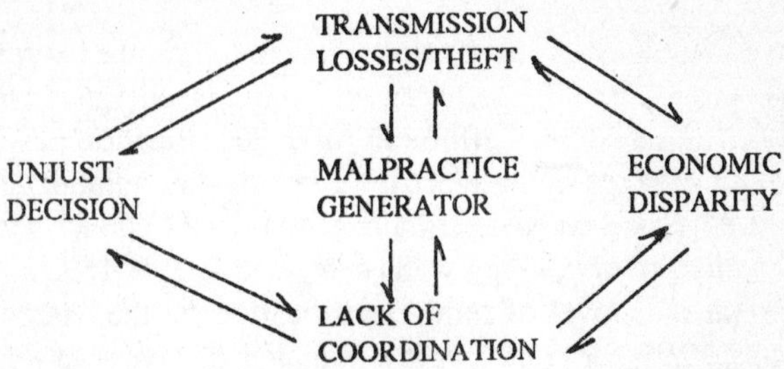

FIG. 6D.2: Consequent Malpractice

About 72 per cent countrymen are involved in agricultural activities which accounts 40 per cent of GNP and 55 per cent of the national export. For this sector 60 per cent of the total power comes from men and animals and rest 40 per cent from mechanical and electrical power, whereas the situation is almost reverse in the industrial sector. To meet the energy problem in the rural sector, there is a vast scope of the use of non-conventional power resources. The use of local sources of power should be promoted by up dating the technology in the field of non conventional energy system development, keeping in view the increasing demand and low purchasing capacity on the one hand and far-flung location of villages on the other. The conventional use of power can be supplemented by the development of biomass-biogas, solar and wind energy abundantly available in Rajasthan.

Villages Electrified

There were 34,533 villages in Rajasthan according to 1961 Census. Out of these, 32,241 villages were inhabited and 2,292 villages were uninhabited. According to 1971 Census, the total number of villages in Rajasthan was 35,795 out of which 33,305 villages were inhabited and 2,490 villages were uninhabited. The total number of village as per 1981 Census increased to 37,124 out of which 34,968 village are inhabited and 2156 villages are uninhabited. The electrification of inhabited villages from the population point of view is given in Table 6D.2.

During the Fifth Plan rural electrification was included in the 'Minimum Needs Programme', reflecting its importance by the Government.The capital costs of rural electrification are quite high and

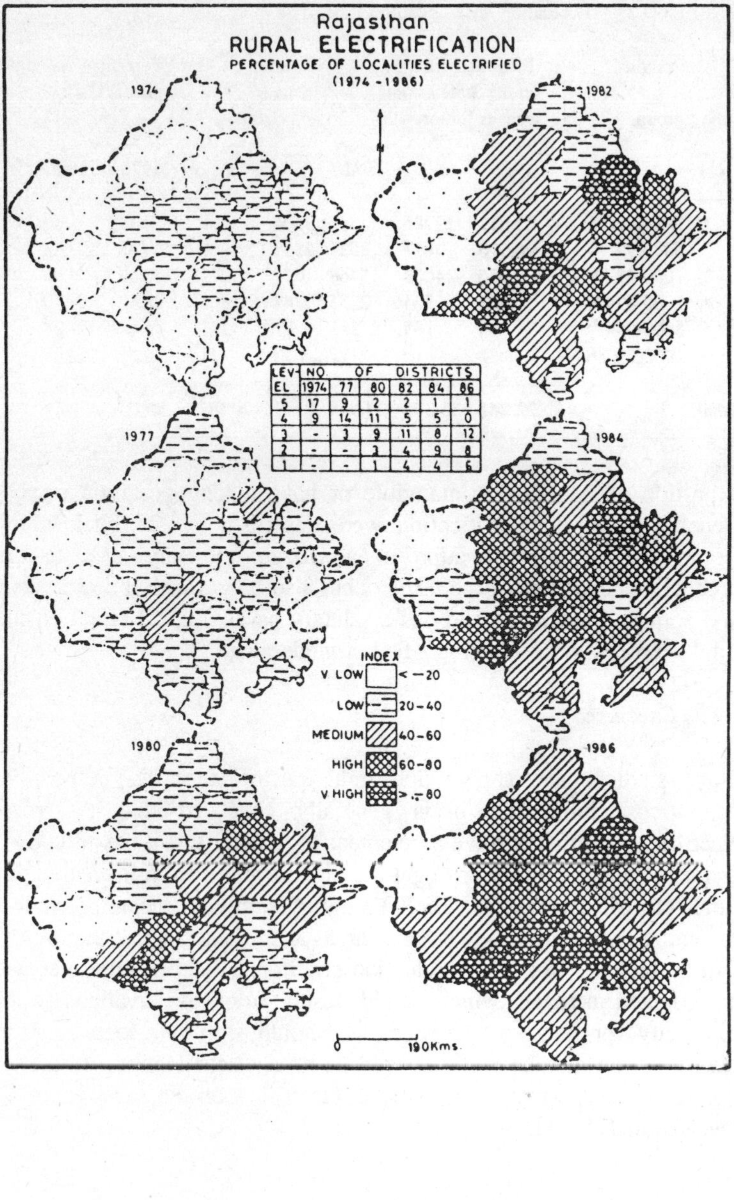

LEVEL	NO. OF DISTRICTS 1974	77	80	82	84	86
5	17	9	2	2	1	1
4	9	14	11	5	5	0
3	-	3	9	11	8	12
2	-	-	3	4	9	8
1	-	-	1	4	4	6

FIG. 6D.3

TABLE 6D.2: Population-wise Localities Electrified

Population group	Inhabited villages in the State as per census Reports			No.of villages electrified		Percentage of electrification	
	1961	1971	1981	1976	1986	1976	1986
1. Below 500	21,612	19781	18286	3504	8661	17.71	47.36
2. 500-999	6,596	7817	8537	2383	5966	30.48	69.88
3. 1000-1999	2,936	4008	5468	1631	4079	40.69	74.60
4. 2000-4999	1,003	1524	2335	744	1861	48.82	79.70
5. 5000-9999	94	165	321	77	293	46.67	91.28
6. 10000 & above	—	10	21	10	21	100.00	100.00
Total	32,241	33,305	34,968	8349	20881	25.07	59.71

a portion of benefits is intangible or have a long gestation period. Benefits of rural electrification were described by the Fuel Policy Committee as "electrification of a village not only adds to the productive capacities of the farmers but also brings with it social, civil and domestic amenities and has a salutary psychological effect on the rural people who start having a feel of modern age."*

Wells Energised

Some studies have shown that rural electrification has a positive benefit-cost ratio, but it is generally conceded that the rural electrification must involve an element of subsidy just it has in U.S.A. and other nations. In order to get the highest return from investment in rural electrification, the Fuel Policy Committee recommended a screening procedure to select those areas and villages where the returns will be highest. One major selection criterion is the potential increase in irrigated acreage which could result from the availability of electricity for pump-sets, hence, we should shift our focus on the electrification of tube wells as well as rural electrification. Rajasthan has made a substantial growth of electrification of tube wells as revealed in Table 6D.3.

* Government of India, "Report of the Fuel Policy Committee," Delhi: Government of India Press, 1975.

TABLE 6D.3: Wells Energised in Rajasthan

Year	No. of wells	Variation	% of variation
1968-69	18,368	—	—
1970-71	35,007	16,639	90.59
1972-73	65,716	30,709	87.72
1974-75	85,323	19,607	29.84
1976-77	107,355	22,032	25.82
1978-79	155,098	47,743	44.47
1980-81	207,435	52,337	33.74
1982-83	244,219	36,784	17.73
1984-85	272,880	28,661	11.73
1986-87	292,804	19,924	7.30

Electrification of Harijan Basties

The scheduled castes and scheduled tribes account for nearly 30 per cent of the population of Rajasthan as per 1981 Census, out of which 88 per cent (8817 thousand) live in villages and only 12 per cent (1204 thousand) live in cities. Rural electrification is a function of providing domestic connections in villages and irrigation connections in cultivable lands. While considering the problem of rural electrification it is essential to take into account the 30 per cent Harijan population of the State of which 88 per cent is rural. These poverty stricken people may not be neglected. Their living style can be improved by providing with electricity supply to their *basties* at cheaper rates as their purchasing power inhibits them to ask for power connection. It is significant to note that substantial efforts have been made in this direction in Rajasthan. The electrification of Harijan Basties is noted in Table 6D.4 and illustrated in Fig. 6D.4.

TABLE 6D.4: Electrification of Harijan Basties

Year	Basties electrified	Annual variation	Per cent variation
1979-80	2810		—
1980-81	3608	798	28.4
1981-82	4584	976	27.1
1982-83	5677	1093	23.8
1983-84	6829	1152	20.3
1984-85	8922	2093	30.6
1985-86	10016	1094	12.3

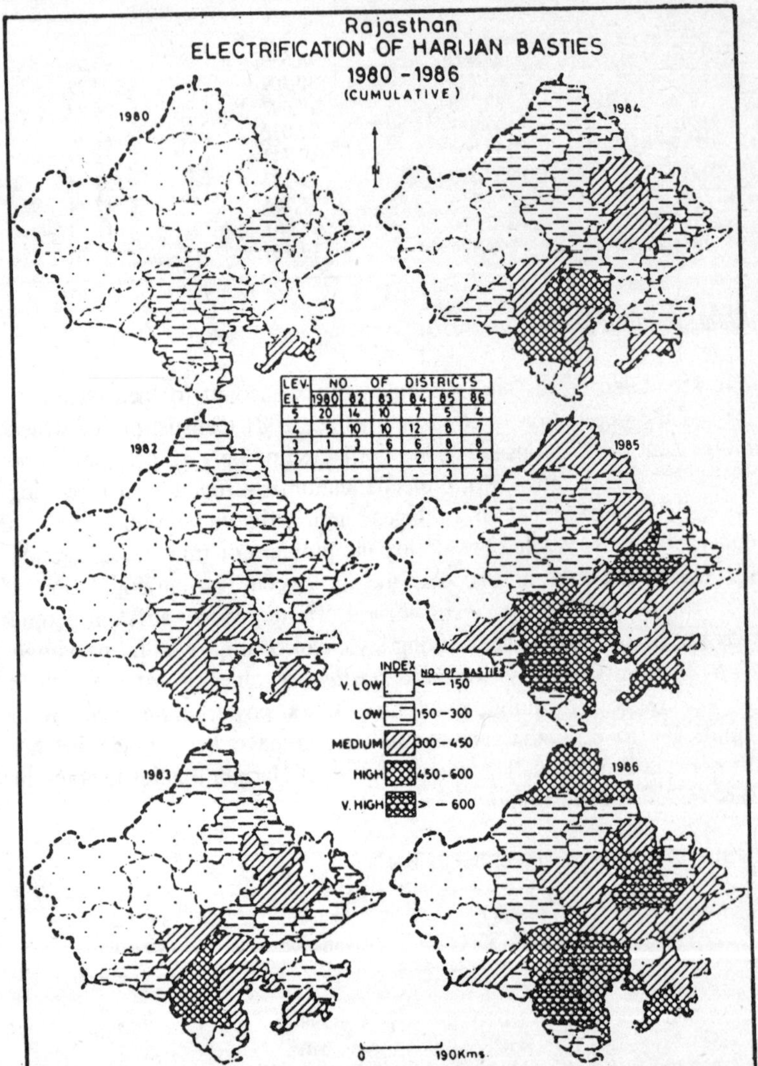

LEVEL	NO. OF DISTRICTS					
	1980	82	83	84	85	86
5	20	14	10	7	5	4
4	5	10	10	12	8	7
3	1	3	6	6	8	8
2	-	-	1	2	3	5
1	-	-	-	-	3	3

FIG. 6D.4

6E. *Income and Expenditure on Power*

Power, as a base for all-round economic development has received massive doses of funds (Rs. 1111.66 crores up to the Sixth Plan) and the Seventh Plan has an outlay for this sector of the order of Rs. 927.48 crores. Table 6E.1 depicts the outlay and expenditure on power during five year plans.

TABLE 6E.1: Outlay and Expenditure on Power in Rajasthan

Plan	Period	Outlay		Expenditure	
		Crore Rs.	% of total	Crore Rs.	% of Total
First	1951-56	9.58	14.85	1.24	2.29
Second	1956-61	19.99	18.99	15.15	14.75
Third	1961-66	35.00	14.83	39.36	18.50
Annual	1966-69	47.29	35.63	46.82	34.24
Fourth	1969-74	90.37	29.51	93.98	30.43
Fifth	1974-79	242.30	28.60	248.97	29.03
Annual	1979-80	90.00	32.73	100.00	34.46
Sixth	1980-85	650.61	32.13	566.14	26.57
Seventh	1985-90	927.48	30..92	126.00	29.30

Source: Budget Study, 1986-87

Massive investments under successive plans have helped to increase power supply rising from 48 mkWh in 1956 to 4808 mkWh in 1986. However, in view of requirements of the economy and position obtaining in adjoining States and at all India level, much more still needs to be done.

Table 6E.2 shows that the power sector in Rajasthan has made substantial profit (before appropriation) to the State income except 1971-72, 1972-73, 1979-80, and 1981-82, the years of deficit. The table also reveals that income and expenditure have been gradually increasing with the rising volume of power generation, the expenditure increased by Rs. 100 crores from Rs. 35 crores in 1971-72 to 135 crores in 1985-86. Whereas the income rose by Rs. 227 crores from Rs. 24 crores in 1971-72 to Rs. 251 in 1985-86 making a profit of Rs. 116 crores to the State. Figure 6E.1 illustrates the same picture. But the illustrations in Fig. 6E.2 exhibit a reverse picture after making an appropriation for payment of debts (Appendix Table 6E.3). The power sector in Rajasthan has registered continuous loss rising from Rs. 2.5 million in 1957-58 to 455.7 million in 1985-86.

TABLE 6E.2: Income and Expenditure on Power before Appropriation (in crores of Rupees)

Year	Expenditure	Income	Difference
1971-72	35	24	–11
1972-73	34	26	–8
1973-74	27	33	+6
1974-75	33	43	+10
1975-76	39	51	+12
1976-77	53	68	+15
1977-78	63	76	+13
1978-79	90	99	+9
1979-80	134	131	–3
1980-81	126	132	+6
1981-82	140	121	–19
1982-83	111	157	+46
1983-84	131	214	+83
1984-85	133	226	+93
1985-86	135	251	+116

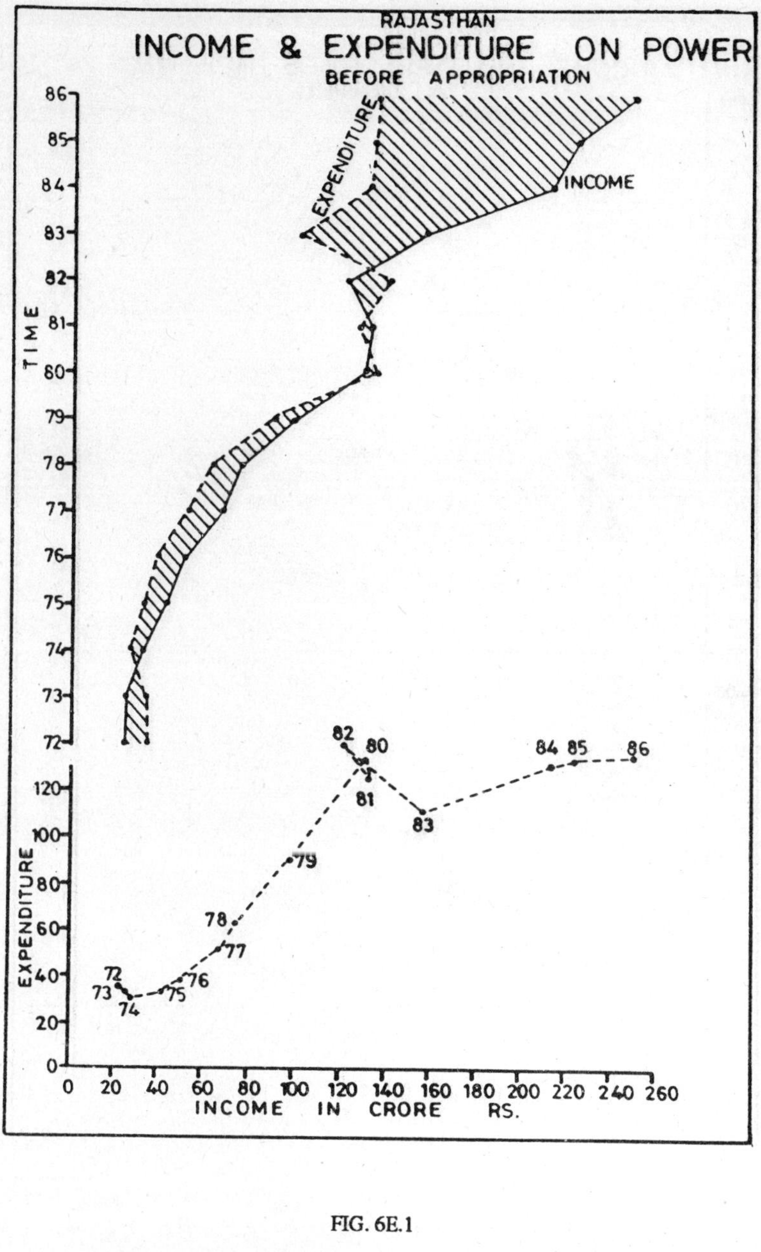
RAJASTHAN
INCOME & EXPENDITURE ON POWER
BEFORE APPROPRIATION
EXPENDITURE
INCOME
TIME
EXPENDITURE
INCOME IN CRORE RS.

FIG. 6E.1

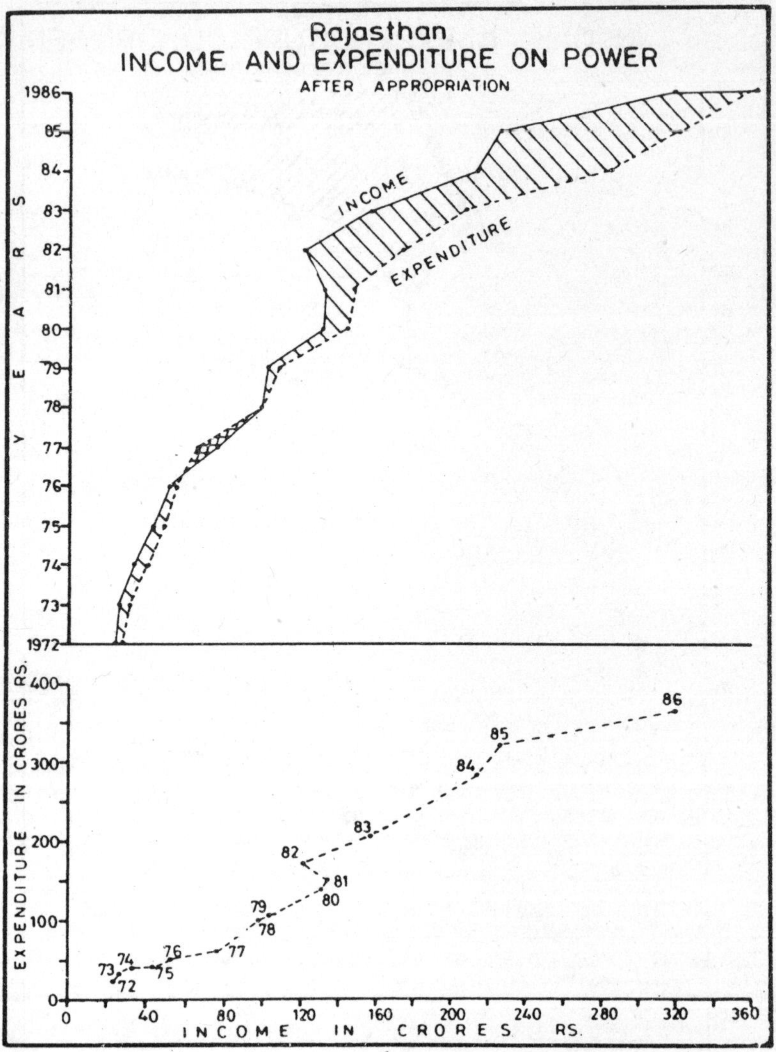
Rajasthan
INCOME AND EXPENDITURE ON POWER
AFTER APPROPRIATION
1986
85
84
83
82
81
80
79
78
77
76
75
74
73
1972
YEARS
INCOME
EXPENDITURE
EXPENDITURE IN CRORES RS.
400
300
200
100
0
86
85
84
83
82
81
80
79
78
77
76
75
74
73
72
0
40
80
120
160
200
240
280
320
360
INCOME IN CRORES RS.

FIG. 6E.2

7

SUMMARY AND CONCLUSIONS

POWER CONSUMPTION in Rajasthan has made substantial growth since the formation of the State in 1949. The consumption depends upon availability of power, which has also made gigantic growth rising from 13 MW in 1948-49 to 1797 MW in 1985-86. The increasing trends in the availability of power have helped to open new vistas of prosperity and living style of the inhabitants of the State. More than 20 thousand villages (62.7% of inhabited villages) have been electrified while there were only 42 electrified localities at the time of the formation of Rajasthan. The per capita consumption of power has increased from 15 kWh in 1965 to 124 kWh in 1986. The aggregate consumption of power has risen from 48 mkWh to 4808 mkWh during the period 1956-57 to 1985-86. The rate of growth of power consumption is computed 11.26 per cent per annum during 1970-71 to 1984-85. A big deficit (4325 MU) still exist between demand (9133 MU) and supply (4808 MU) in spite of this growth, and it will continue in near future. The situation can be remedied by augmenting the existing installed capacity as well as creating new avenues to perennial sources of power.

There has been a remarkable shift in the pattern of consumption of electricity particularly over the past two decades. Agriculture and irrigation is the second largest consumer, being next to industrial sector. As against 4.2 per cent being utilized for agricultural and irrigation purposes, in 1957-58, the proportion has gone up to 30.23 per cent in 1985-86. Even in 1981-82, this proportion was 32.77 per cent. In contrast to this increasing trend in agricultural power consumption, the industrial sector tended to decrease its proportion once attained of the order of 58.96 per cent in 1977-78, which declined to 45.93 per cent in 1985-86 (Table 3B.3 in Chapter 3). Industries and agriculture have been consuming more than 75 per cent of power – budget of the State since 1970. During 1957-58, the industrial sector shared 35.65 per cent of State's total power followed by water-supply sector

(21.57%), domestic sector (16.81%), commercial sector (16.21%), agriculture and irrigation sector (4.21%) and street-lighting (5.55%). Whereas, during 1985-86, the industrial sector shared 45.93 per cent followed by agriculture (30.23%), domestic sector (9.63%), commercial sector (5.41%), water supply sector (5.01%), mix load consumers (3.11%) and the street-lighting (0.68%) at the tail-end.

The study concludes that the economic development (in terms of NSDP) of Rajasthan has been strongly correlated ($r=0.962$, $R^2=0.926$ and $t=12.88$) with increases in the use of energy (in terms of NSPC). Indeed, when per capita power consumption and per capita income are plotted against each other (Fig. 7B.2) the resulting points fall within a fairly narrow band. Agricultural sector (52.22%) and industrial sector (21.47%) dominate the economy, as they shared 73.69 per cent of the Net State Domestic Product consuming 76.16 per cent of Net State Power consumption in 1985-86. Hence the levels of electrification and the levels of per capita power consumption are considered the levels of economic development.

7A. Levels of Electrification in Rajasthan

The main objective of the present study was to assess the levels of electrification in Rajasthan at district level. For this purpose six cumulative variables have been taken into consideration since the formation of the State till the last data were obtained in 1986. The actual number of power consumers ($\times 1$), amount of power consumption ($\times 2$), transformers installed KVA capacity ($\times 3$), number of localities electrified so far ($\times 4$), number of basties of ST and SC electrified so far ($\times 5$), and the number of wells energised so far ($\times 6$) have been computed into standardised values applying the formula $SV=X-\overline{X}^2/SD$. A composite index $(\Sigma X/n)$ for all the 27 districts of the State has been reckoned through the computation so as to assess the levels of electrification. All the districts have been classified into five levels of electrification on the basis of the composite index computed in Appendix Table 7A.1. The following equations were obtained through the calculations.

$$\times 1 = X-76.94/61.93 \quad (7.1)$$
$$\times 2 = X-178.07/175.87 \quad (7.2)$$
$$\times 3 = X-382.55/336.87 \quad (7.3)$$
$$\times 4 = X-773.37/432.22 \quad (7.4)$$

$$\times 5 = X\text{-}371.18/212.11 \tag{7.5}$$
$$\times 6 = X\text{-}10443.90/10718.80 \tag{7.6}$$

Very High Level of Electrification: According to our analysis, out of 27 districts of Rajasthan, only two districts namely, Jaipur and Udaipur, were recorded in very high level of electrification accounting for the index value of more than one. Jaipur district alone shared almost 16 per cent each of the consumers, consumption and kVA installed capacity of the State's total which was more than four times higher than the State's average. Whereas in Udaipur district 6.2 per cent of State's total number of power consumers, utilized almost 10 per cent of State's total power with 5.76 installed kVA capacity. The district accounted nearly 8 per cent for State's rural and poor *basties'* electrification. These two districts having 22.3 per cent of State's total number of consumers, utilized almost 26 per cent of State's total power.

High Level of Electrification: Five districts were recorded in highly electrified level namely, Alwar, Bhilwara, Chittorgarh, Sikar and Kota. Kota district utilized 10.52 per cent of State's total power for its 5.46 per cent consumers. Alwar district consumed 7.59 per cent power for 4.28 per cent State's consumers. Bhilwara district consumed 3.19 per cent energy for 3.74 per cent consumers having highest (9.32%) electrification of Harijan Basties in the State. Whereas, 3.97 per cent of State's total consumers used 4.11 per cent of State's total power in Chittorgarh district and 5.22 per cent power was utilized by 4.94 per cent consumers in Sikar. These five districts utilize 30.63 per cent of State's total power for its 22.39 per cent consumers with 31.33 per cent of installed transformer's kVA capacity covering nearly 28 per cent electrified villages and 30 per cent tube wells energised in the State.

Medium Level of Electrification: Six districts were computed in the medium level. These districts are Ajmer, Jhunjhunu, Jodhpur, Nagor, Pali and Sri Ganganagar. About 30 per cent of State's power consumers utilized almost 26 per cent energy in this category having 23 per cent transforms kVA capacity. These districts covered 22 per cent of State's electrified villages and nearly 23 per cent energised tube-wells.

Low Level of Electrification: Five districts namely, Bharatpur, Jalore, Jhalawar, Sawai Madhopur and Sirohi were recorded in the low level of electrification taking into consideration the six variables of the power sector. Bharatpur district served 2.76 per cent consumers with

1.56 per cent of power at an installed transformer capacity of 3.28 per cent covering 3.73 per cent rural electrification and 2.77 per cent energisation of wells. Jalore district consumed 1.97 per cent power for 1.96 per cent of State's consumers. Jhalawar utilized only 0.92 per cent energy for 1.85 per cent State's consumers. Swai Madhopur district served 2.83 per cent consumers with 2.33 per cent power and Sirohi district used 2.62 per cent State's power for its 1.93 per cent consumers. At an aggregate all these five districts shared 9.4 per cent State's power supply for its 11.33 per cent consumers and covered 15.64 per cent of electrified villages, 15.82 per cent of energised wells and 20.33 per cent of the State's poor localities electrification. It can be emphasised here that the percentage of localities electrified, wells energised and consumers served, was greater in respect to the amount of power utilized in these districts. And this caused the low level of electrification of these districts.

Very Low Level of Electrification: Eight districts covering about 28 per cent area and 18 per cent population of the State, were computed in very low level of electrification. These districts are Barmer, Banswara, Bikaner, Bundi, Churu, Dholpur, Dungarpur and Tonk. About 7 per cent of State's total power supply was utilized for almost 14 per cent of its consumers with 11 per cent installed transformer kVA capacity covering 17 per cent electrified villages, 15.4 per cent poor *basties* and 6.49 per cent of tube-wells energised.

Negligible Electrification: Jaisalmer district covering 11.22 per cent area and 0.7 per cent population of the State, consumed only 0.26 per cent electricity for its 0.27 per cent consumers with 0.16 per cent transformers installed kVA capacity. Figure 7A.1 illustrates the levels of electrification in Rajasthan.

7B. Levels of Per Capita Power Consumption

Power is one of the most important infrastructural necessities for sound economic development. Economic development of Rajasthan is conditioned to a great extent by the availability of suitable quantity of power since the State has diverse levels of per head power utilization. Fig. 7B.1 shows five levels of per capita power consumption in Rajasthan for six points of time viz., 1974, 1976, 1978, 1980, 1982 and 1985 on the basis of availability of district-wise data, is an attempt to assess the growth trends of power in the State.

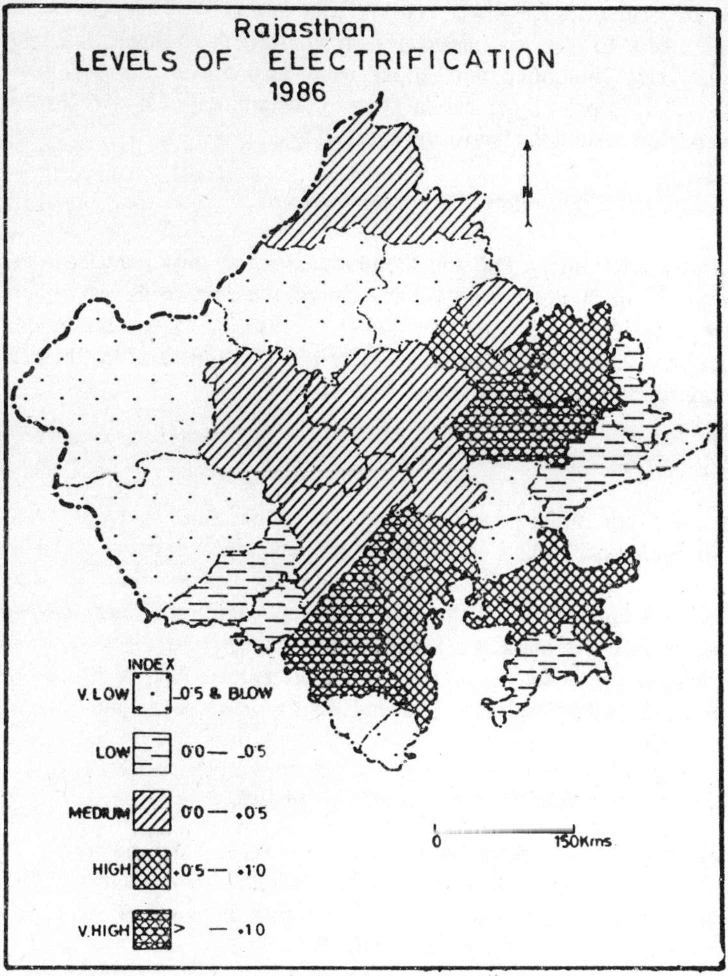

FIG. 7A.1

Levels of Per Capita Power Consumption in 1974

A majority of 19 districts exhibited very poor (below 50 kWh) per capita power consumption in 1974. Out of the remaining seven districts, Kota was the only district which accounted very high (above 200 kWh) per capita power consumption in terms of average of the State. Rest of the six districts namely Ajmer, Jodhpur, Udaipur, Chittorgarh, Jhunjhunu and Jaipur were recorded in the low level (50-100 kWh/pc) of per capita power consumption. All the districts except Kota, remained below the national average.

Levels of Per Capita Power Consumption in 1976

Two districts namely, Pali and Jhunjhunu made an improvement in per capita use of power during the two years, the first rising from Very Low Level (<50 kWh) to Low Level (50-100 kWh) and the second from Low Level to Medium Level (100-150 kWh). Rest of the districts remained in their same groups as were in 1974.

Levels of Per Capita Power Consumption in 1978

The mean per capita power consumption for the State as a whole was of the order of 74.32 kWh in 1978 and seventeen districts remained below to it. Kota was first order per capita power consumer utilizing four times higher (303.9) the State's average. Jaipur, Chittorgarh and Udaipur districts made an improvement rising from Low Level to Medium Level. Whereas, Bikaner improved its level from Very Low to Low Level, while Jodhpur, Pali and Ajmer districts remained in the same group.

Levels of Per Capita Power Consumption in 1980

Very High Level – Kota district continued to consume maximum per capita power in spite of a decline from 303.9 kWh in 1978 to 277.1 kWh in 1979-80. It was still three times higher the mean of State's per capita consumption (93.1 kWh) during the year.

High Level – Jaipur, Udaipur and Jhunjhunu districts continued to improve their level making a jump from Medium Level (100-150 kWh) to High Level (150-200 kWh). Jhunjhunu district consumed maximum per capita power (172 kWh) in this group followed by Udaipur (159.1 kWh) and Jaipur (157.2 kWh).

Medium Level – Four districts namely, Sikar, Ajmer, Pali and Chittorgarh were recorded in this group in 1980. Sikar and Ajmer districts made a long jump rising from Very Low Level to Medium Level.

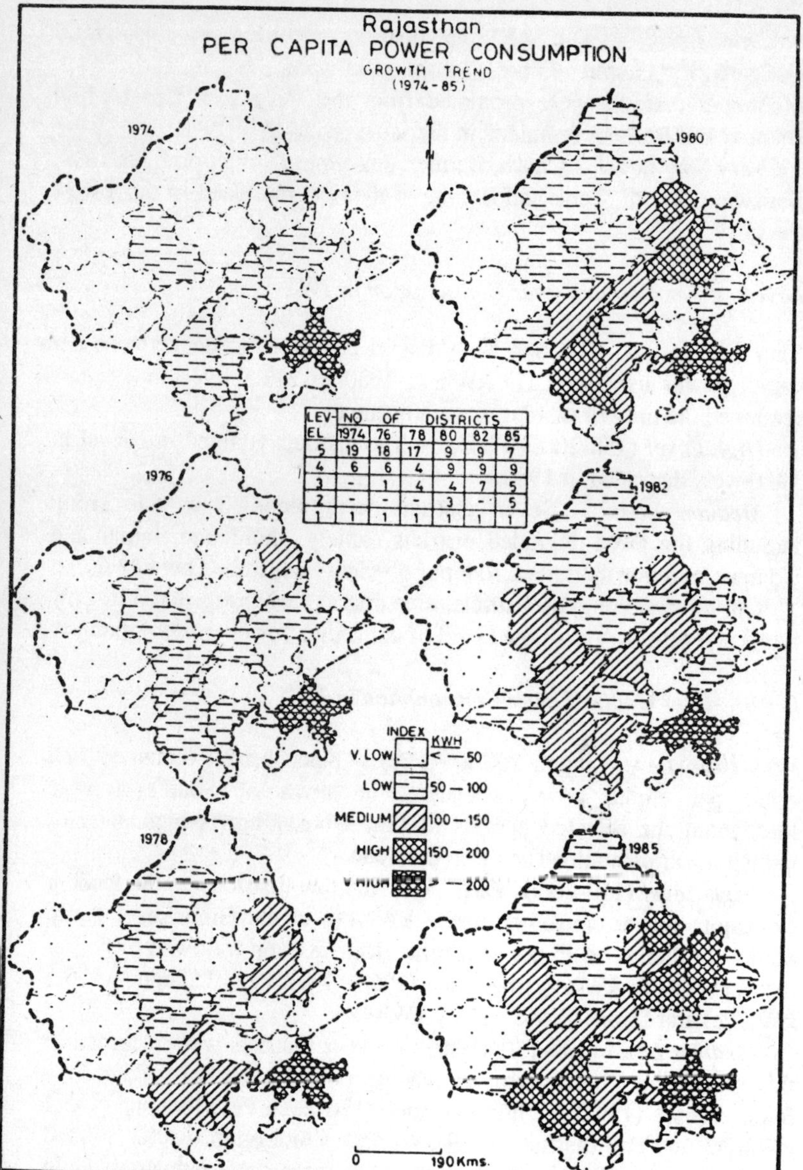

LEVEL	NO OF DISTRICTS					
	1974	76	78	80	82	85
5	19	18	17	9	9	7
4	6	6	4	9	9	9
3	-	1	4	4	7	5
2	-	-	-	3	-	5
1	1	1	1	1	1	1

FIG. 7B.1

Low Level – Out of nine districts recorded in this group Ganganagar, Nagor, Jalore, Sirohi, Bhilwara, Alwar and Sawai Madhopur districts were promoted from the Very Low Level while Bikaner and Jodhpur remained in the same group as in 1978.

Very Low Level – Churu, Barmer, Jaisalmer, Dungarpur, Jhalawar, Banswara, Bundi, Tonk and Bharatpur districts remained in the lowest category.

Levels of Per Capita Power Consumption in 1982

Very High Level – Though Kota district continued to decrease its per capita power use from 277 kWh in 1980 to 217.8 kWh in 1982, it remained the only first order power consumer.

High Level (150-200 kWh/Pc) – The districts attained this level in 1980 were degraded in 1982.

Medium Level – Seven districts were recorded in this group including the three degraded districts namely, Jhunjhunu, Jaipur and Udaipur, and one upgraded, Jodhpur district rising from Low Level.

Out of remaining 18 districts, nine districts were registered in Low Level and nine in Very Low Level of per capita power consumption.

Levels of Per Capita Power Consumption in 1985

Very High Level (above 200 kWh/Pc) – Kota district remained first order per capita power consumer in terms of State's average throughout the selected periods of time envisaging its high level of industrialisation attained so far in the State.

High Level (150-200 kWh/Pc) – Jhunjhunu district was the leading per capita power consumer (199.4 kWh/Pc) in the High Level group obviously due to its 95 per cent rural electrification followed by Jaipur district (197.6 kWh/Pc), Alwar (176.9 kWh/Pc), Udaipur (170.5 kWh/Pc) and Sirohi district (164.7 kWh/Pc).

Medium Level (100-150 kWh/Pc) – Five districts were recorded in this group and Chittorgarh was leading (149.8 kWh/Pc) followed by Sikar district (139.2 kWh/Pc), Ajmer (136 kWh/Pc), Jodhpur (115.2 kWh/Pc) and Pali district (103.9 kWh/Pc). Chittorgarh district utilized its 54 per cent (106.281 mkWh) power in large scale industries while Sikar district consumed 81.48 per cent (204.222 mkWh) of its total power in agriculture. It is interesting to note that 100 per cent rural electrification in Sikar district has witnessed tremendous growth in agricultural power consumption rather the domestic sector.

Low Level (50-100 kWh/Pc) – Nine districts namely Bundi (99.3 kWh/Pc), Bhilwara (88.2 kWh/Pc), Jalore (87.3 kWh/Pc), Sri Ganganagar (79.6 kWh/Pc), Nagor (74.6 kWh/Pc), Bikaner (74.4 kWh/Pc), Sawai Madhopur (69.4 kWh/Pc), Jhalawar (58.8 kWh/Pc) and Bharatpur (52.5 kWh/Pc) were recorded in this group in 1985.

Very Low Level (Below 50 kWh/Pc) – Figure 7B.1 reveal the fact that during the 12 years' period from 1974 to 1985, seven districts continued to remain in the very low level of per capita power consumption. These districts are: Tonk (34.9 kWh/Pc), Barmer (31.8 kWh/Pc), Churu (30.5 kWh/Pc), Jaisalmer (30.4 kWh/Pc), Banswara (29.3 kWh/Pc), Dungarpur (26.6kWh/Pc) and Dholpur (21.7 kWh/Pc). These are most backward, remote and underdeveloped districts of the State. Dholpur is the poorest per capita power consumer district and Kota is the richest. The poorest consumes 13.6 times less than that of the richest. It can be emphasised here that one inhabitant of Kota district uses as much electricity as 14 inhabitants of Dholpur district as per 1985 power-statistics of the State.

Power and Progress of Rajasthan

Economic development of Rajasthan considered in terms of Net State Domestic Product, is closely related to the power consumption. The relationship between economic growth and energy utilization in Rajasthan has been examined to see if it remains constant over time. To explore this relationship between power and progress of the area under study, data regarding Net State Domestic Product (NSDP) and Net State Power Consumption (NSPC) as well as per capita NSDP and NSPC have been taken into consideration for fifteen years from 1972 to 1986. During this period the NSDP increased by Rs. 6456.3 crores rising from Rs. 1464.33 crores in 1971-72 to Rs. 7920.63 crores in 1985-86. Whereas, the NSPC (Net State Power Consumption) increased by 3703.555 mkWh growing from 1104.456 mkWh in 1971-72 to 4808.011 mkWh in 1985-86. The NSDP registered 5.4 fold growth as against 4.4 fold growth of NSPC during the fifteen years taken under observation. Similarly, the per capita NSDP income exhibited 3.5 fold growth as against 3 fold growth of per capita NSPC.

Scatter diagram illustrated in Fig. 7B.2 shows high degree of positive correlation between per capita income and per capita power consumption, because the plotted points of income and power for 15 years tended to lie nearer to the straight line. The graph obtained joining the points of the variables reveals the same result.

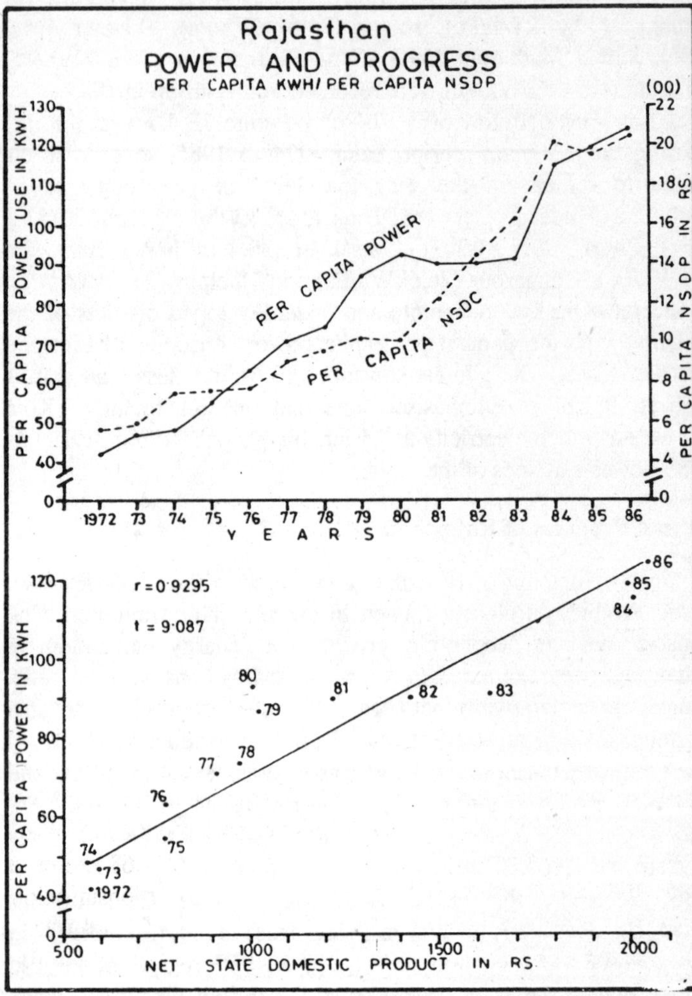

FIG. 7B.2

Figure 7B.3 again displays a scatter diagram and a graph showing the high degree of correlation between Net State Domestic Product and Net State Power Consumption. But these scatter diagrams and the graphs give an intuitive idea about the relationship between income and power consumption. A more precise quantitative measurement of the degree and direction of a linear correlation suggested by Karl Pearson, has been applied.

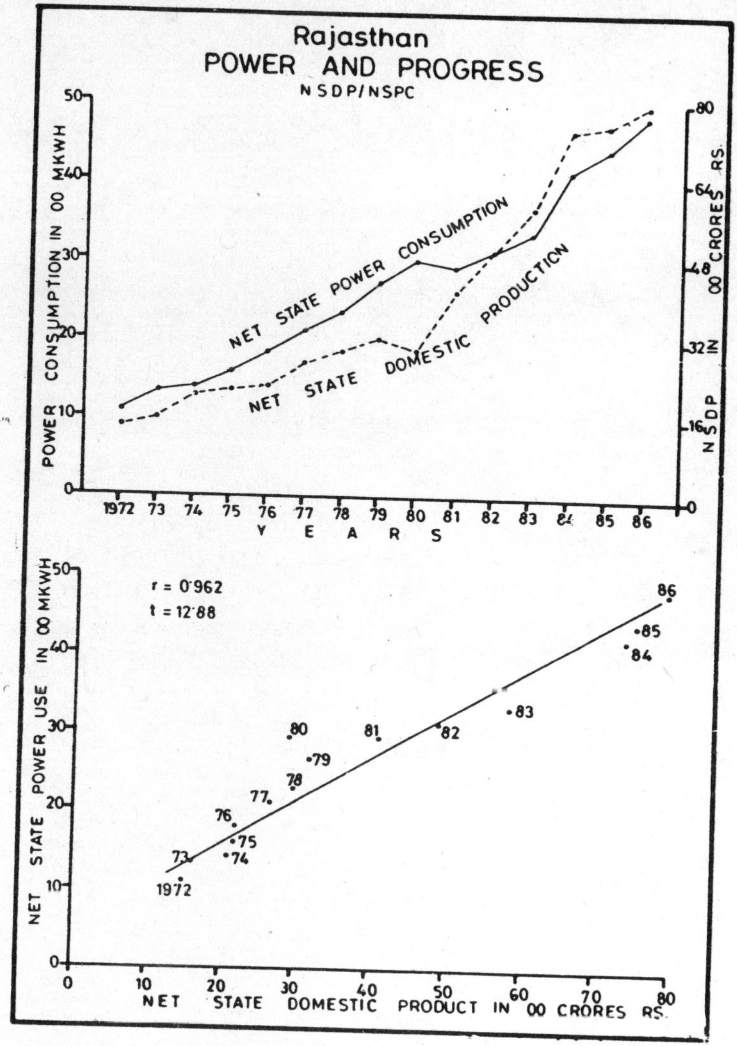

FIG. 7B.3

The results show that there exist a high degree positive relationship between per capita power consumption and the per capita income. The computed correlation coefficient was 0.9295 and applying the test of significance the '*t*' was obtained 9.087 (Appendix Table 7.B). Hence the per capita income and power use are strongly correlated.

APPENDIX TABLE 3B.8: Computation of Growth Rate and Demand of Power in Rajasthan

Time		Domestic		Commercial		Industrial		Agriculture		Pub. Light		Water Supply		Mix Load		Aggregate	
t	*t2*	*Log Y*	*t Log Y*	*Log Y*	*t Log Y*	*Log Y*	*t Log Y*	*Log Y*	*t Log Y*	*Log Y*	*t Log Y*	*Log Y*	*t Log Y*	*Log Y*	*t Log Y*	*Log Y*	*t Log Y*
(1971)																	
-7	49	1.7787	-12.4509	1.6945	-11.8614	2.7795	-19.4565	2.0477	-14.3344	0.9388	-6.5787	1.7560	-12.2917	1.8461	-12.9224	2.982	-20.872
-6	36	1.8505	-11.1030	1.7671	-10.6027	2.8429	-17.0577	2.1866	-13.1198	0.9922	-5.9532	1.7592	-10.5552	1.7604	-10.5626	3.043	-18.259
-5	25	1.9116	-9.5580	1.8099	-9.0499	2.8764	-14.3819	2.3592	-11.7962	1.0877	-5.4385	1.3231	- 9.1157	1.7457	- 8.7283	3.101	-15.505
-4	16	1.9549	-7.8197	1.8181	-7.2722	2.8782	-11.5129	2.4467	- 9.7867	1.0793	-4.3173	1.3896	- 7.5584	1.7058	- 6.8232	3.124	-12.497
-3	9	2.0113	-6.0338	1.9046	-5.7137	2.9395	- 8.8186	2.5382	- 7.6147	1.0824	-3.2472	1.9232	- 5.7697	1.8466	- 5.5399	3.194	- 9.593
-2	4	2.0779	-4.1559	1.9651	-3.9302	3.0380	- 6.0760	2.5481	- 5.0962	1.1564	-2.3128	1.9602	- 3.9204	1.7815	- 3.5630	3.261	- 6.521
-1	1	2.1287	-2.1287	2.0235	-2.0235	3.0932	- 3.0932	2.6333	- 2.6333	1.1821	-1.1821	2.0112	- 2.0112	1.9053	-1.9053	3.324	- 3.324
0	0	2.1998	0	2.0739	0	3.1262	0	2.6517	0	1.2573	0	2.0557	0	1.8675	0	3.355	0
1	1	2.2504	2.2504	2.1188	2.1188	3.1923	3.1923	2.8033	2.8033	1.2925	1.2925	2.0851	2.0851	1.9104	1.9104	3.435	3.435
2	4	2.3103	4.6207	2.1464	4.2928	3.1676	6.3352	2.9619	5.9238	1.3080	2.6161	2.1250	4.2499	1.9238	3.8476	3.473	6.945
3	9	2.3460	7.0379	2.1568	6.4704	3.1121	9.3363	3.0021	9.0064	1.2908	3.8724	2.1746	6.5239	1.9783	5.9349	3.467	10.400
4	16	2.4127	9.6509	2.2095	8.8379	3.1454	12.5816	3.0112	12.0449	1.2592	5.0367	2.1985	8.7940	2.0452	8.1808	3.496	13.983
5	25	2.4699	12.3496	2.2710	11.3549	3.1141	15.5707	3.0724	15.3619	1.3546	6.7731	2.2324	11.1621	2.0483	10.2413	3.514	17.572
6	36	2.5317	15.1906	2.2931	13.7589	3.2985	19.7912	3.1145	18.6868	1.3831	8.2989	2.2573	13.5437	2.0680	12.4081	3.618	21.707
7	49	2.6074	18.2516	2.3561	16.4930	3.2975	23.0827	3.1449	22.0143	1.4671	10.2699	2.3391	16.3736	2.1035	14.7246	3.642	25.495
(1985)																	
Total	280	32.8418	16.1017	30.6884	12.8731	45.3014	9.4937	40.5219	21.4599	18.1325	9.1299	30.5902	11.5099	28.5364	7.2028	50.029	12.9764

(*Contd.*)

(*Contd.*)

Time	Domestic	Commercial	Industrial	Agriculture	Pub. Light	Water Supply	Mix Load	Aggregate
t $t2$	*Log Y* *t Log Y*	*Log Y* *t Log Y*	*Log Y* *t Log Y*	*Log Y* *t Log Y*	*Log Y* *t Log Y*	*Log Y* *t Log Y*	*Log Y* *t Log Y*	*Log Y* *t Log Y*
$a = \frac{\Sigma Log\ Y}{N}$	2.1895	2.0459	3.06009	2.7014	1.2088	2.0393	1.9024	3.3353
$b = \frac{\Sigma t\ Log\ Y}{t^2}$	0.0575061	0.0459753	0.0339041	0.0766427	0.0332607	0.0411067	0.0257244	0.0463442
Growth rate = ALb -1×100/	14.15%	11.16%	8.11%	19.3%	7.79%	9.93%	6.10%	11.26%
Log Y=a+b×t 1990	757.832	395.916	2930.483	3160.953	39.818	340.489	162.589	7788.080
1995	1469.277	672.171	4329.719	5984.505	57.959	556.309	218.633	13278.573
2000 (mkWh)	2848.618	1141.186	6397.056	10998.029	84.363	876.545	293.993	22639.790

APPENDIX TABLE 4.1: Growth of Power Consumption in Rajasthan (in mkWh)

Years	Domestic	Commercial	Industrial	Street light	Irrigation	Public w/v	Others	Total
1956-57	8.139	7.844	17.251	2.686	2.032	10.438	—	48.390
1957-58	8.568	8.261	18.168	2.828	2.141	10.993	—	50.959
1958-59	10.498	8.138	17.620	2.557	1.979	12.312	—	53.104
1959-60	11.679	10.230	13.607	2.149	3.824	12.676	—	54.135
1960-61	13.031	12.877	19.268	3.237	6.363	14.684	—	69.460
1961-62	17.25	17.05	25.51	4.29	8.42	19.45	—	91.970
1962-63	24.79	19.58	59.05	4.96	9.11	21.89	—	139.380
1963-64	22.63	19.95	168.14	5.16	13.12	25.34	2.67	257.010
1964-65	27.973	27.059	234.312	6.843	10.055	23.506	50.240	379.988
1965-66	30.03	27.62	192.65	6.19	19.14	21.07	35.52	332.220
1966-67	30.83	32.41	162.26	6.50	28.65	29.05	34.28	323.980
1967-68	37.248	37.535	218.575	7.410	36.864	31.974	37.993	407.599
1968-69	42.459	40.487	397.177	8.239	67.221	45.347	50.096	651.026
1969-70	52.833	45.550	467.248	8.595	89.644	52.635	68.773	785.278
1970-71	60.077	49.486	601.858	8.706	111.629	57.012	70.156	958.924
1971-72	70.875	58.494	696.536	9.822	153.688	57.439	57.602	1104.456
1972-73	81.582	64.562	752.289	12.238	228.686	66.548	55.676	1261.581
1973-74	90.144	65.775	755.498	12.004	279.689	77.556	50.794	1331.460
1974-75	102.628	80.274	870.040	12.089	345.330	83.800	70.249	1564.410
1975-76	119.664	92.274	1091.425	14.335	353.245	91.247	60.466	1822.656
1976-77	134.500	105.562	1239.235	15.208	429.882	102.604	80.405	2107.396
1977-78	158.433	118.542	1337.065	18.084	448.447	113.696	73.713	2267.980
1978-79	177.978	131.449	1556.992	19.612	635.777	121.658	81.355	2724.821
1979-80	204.330	140.089	1470.952	20.326	916.040	133.348	83.910	2968.995
1980-81	221.815	143.488	1294.550	19.535	1004.948	149.497	95.128	2928.961
1981-82	258.667	161.990	1397.511	18.163	1026.162	157.940	110.968	3131.401
1982-83	295.065	186.630	1300.603	22.627	1181.337	170.774	111.753	3268.789
1983-84	340.223	196.401	1988.555	24.163	1301.580	180.834	116.954	4148.710
1984-85	404.929	227.061	1983.935	29.318	1396.080	218.316	126.916	4386.555
1985-86	463.180	260.249	2208.188	32.531	1453.643	240.698	149.522	4808.011
1986-87	539.442	282.147	2511.096	30.763	1580.040	264.854	185.574	5393.916
1987-88	639.041	319.401	2430.716	37.193	1811.069	280.390	218.787	5736.597

APPENDIX TABLE 4A.8: Household Power Consumption Trends

Districts	1979-80		1984-85		1989-90	
	mkWh	% of total	mkWh	% of total	mkWh	% of total
1. Ajmer	16.424	8.0	30.677	7.8	44.930	7.4
2. Alwar	6.897	3.4	14.877	3.7	22.857	3.8
3. Banswara	3.058	1.5	5.274	1.3	7.490	1.2
4. Barmer	1.613	0.8	3.756	0.9	6.857	1.1
5. Bharatpur	6.947	3.4	11.070	3.4	13.129	2.2
6. Bhilwara	4.826	2.4	11.276	2.8	20.974	3.5
7. Bikaner	10.473	5.1	16.255	4.0	22.037	3.6
8. Bundi	2.019	1.0	4.097	1.0	6.283	1.1
9. Chittor	4.474	2.2	9.503	2.3	15.642	2.6
10. Churu	5.439	2.7	10.272	2.5	15.105	2.5
11. Dungarpur	2.214	1.1	4.135	1.0	6.056	1.0
12. Jaipur	53.076	26.0	103.105	25.5	153.134	25.2
13. Jaisalmer	0.580	0.3	1.060	0.2	1.540	0.3
14. Jalore	1.365	0.7	2.981	0.7	4.597	0.8
15. Jhalawar	2.546	1.3	5.177	1.3	7.808	1.3
16. Jhunjhunu	3.952	1.9	8.432	2.1	12.912	2.1
17. Jodhpur	15.518	7.6	28.350	7.0	41.182	6.8
18. Kota	14.433	7.1	32.134	7.9	49.835	8.2
19. Nagor	4.917	2.4	10.082	2.5	15.247	2.5
20. Pali	4.831	2.4	10.602	2.6	16.373	2.7
21. S. Madhopur	3.359	1.6	7.511	1.8	11.663	1.9
22. Sikar	5.764	2.8	13.529	3.3	21.294	3.5
23. Sirohi	2.440	1.2	4.503	1.1	6.566	1.1
24. Sri Ganganagar	13.099	6.4	26.952	6.7	40.805	6.7
25. Tonk	2.289	1.1	4.605	1.1	6.921	1.1
26. Udaipur	11.767	5.7	23.714	5.9	35.661	5.9
Total	204.320	100	404.929	100	606.868	100

APPENDIX TABLE 4B.3: Spatial Trends of Commercial Power Use

Districts	1979-80		1984-85		Variation	1989-90	
	mkWh	% of total	mkWh	% of total	mkWh	mkWh	% of total
1. Ajmer	10.978	7.8	15.319	6.90	4.341	19.660	6.26
2. Alwar	4.466	3.2	7.852	3.50	3.386	11.238	3.58
3. Banswara	2.264	1.6	4.468	1.98	2.204	6.672	2.12
4. Barmer	1.197	0.8	2.604	1.15	1.407	4.011	1.28
5. Bharatpur	3.558	2.6	6.512	2.80	2.924	9.436	3.00
6. Bhilwara	3.351	2.4	6.193	2.73	2.842	9.035	2.88
7. Bikaner	5.512	3.9	8.697	3.83	3.185	11.882	3.78
8. Bundi	1.566	1.1	2.229	0.98	0.663	2.892	0.92
9. Chittorgarh	2.863	2.1	4.711	2.07	1.848	6.559	2.09
10. Churu	2.144	1.5	3.155	1.39	1.011	4.166	1.33
11. Dungarpur	1.066	0.8	1.826	0.80	0.760	2.586	0.83
12. Jaipur	40.293	28.7	67.469	29.72	27.176	94.645	30.14
13. Jaisalmer	0.552	0.4	0.723	0.31	0.171	0.894	0.28
14. Jalore	0.880	0.6	1.343	0.59	0.463	1.806	0.58
15. Jhalawar	1.629	1.1	2.586	1.14	0.957	3.543	1.13
16. Jhunjhunu	1.738	1.2	2.821	1.24	1.083	3.904	1.24
17. Jodhpur	10.542	7.5	16.922	7.45	6.380	23.302	7.42
18. Kota	9.717	6.9	15.594	6.87	5.877	21.471	6.84
19. Nagor	2.707	1.9	4.058	1.78	1.351	5.409	1.72
20. Pali	4.389	3.2	8.926	3.93	4.537	13.463	4.29
21. S. Madhopur	3.135	2.2	4.596	2.02	1.461	6.057	1.93
22. Sikar	2.508	1.8	4.381	1.93	1.873	6.254	1.99
23. Sirohi	2.310	1.6	3.671	1.62	1.361	5.032	1.60
24. Sri Ganganagar	8.380	6.0	12.604	5.55	4.224	16.828	5.36
25. Tonk	1.850	1.4	2.885	1.27	1.035	3.920	1.25
26. Udaipur	10.464	7.5	14.907	6.56	4.443	19.350	6.16
Total	140.089	100.0	227.052	100.00	86.963	314.015	100.00
<3%		17		17			16
3-4%		3		3			3
>4%		6		6			7

APPENDIX TABLE 4C.4: Levels of Industrial Development in Rajasthan, 1981 (Standardised values of variables and the computation of composite index.

District	X1	X2	X3	X4	X5	Gross	Composite index
1. Ajmer	+1.24	+ .07	+ .89	+ .32	+ .31	+2.83	+ .566
2. Alwar	- .29	+ .35	- .22	- .17	- .23	- .56	- .112
3. Banswara	- .63	- .52	- .46	- .53	- .49	-2.63	- .526
4. Barmer	- .67	- .64	- .49	- .58	- .54	-2.92	- .584
5. Bharatpur	- .13	- .32	- .12	+ .08	- .02	- .51	- .102
6. Bhilwara	+ .12	- .11	+ .25	+ .27	+ .23	+ .76	+ .152
7. Bikaner	- .05	- .52	- .19	- .34	- .34	-1.44	- .288
8. Bundi	- .52	- .59	- .23	- .51	- .48	-2.33	- .466
9. Chittor	- .37	+ .38	- .29	- .06	- .05	- .39	- .078
10. Churu	- .56	- .58	- .53	- .53	- .51	-2.71	- .542
11. Dungarpur	- .76	- .64	- .56	- .66	- .59	- .32	- .642
12. Jaipur	+ .532	+1.04	+4.33	+4.00	+4.07	+16.96	+3.392
13. Jaisalmer	- .76	- .66	- .57	- .64	- .59	-3.22	- .644
14. Jalore	- .75	- .64	- .55	- .63	- .58	-3.15	- .630
15. Jhalawar	- .69	- .47	- .56	- .64	- .59	-2.95	- .590
16. Jhunjhunu	- .73	+ .64	- .33	- .06	- .05	- .53	- .106
17. Jodhpur	+1.11	- .29	+ .18	+ .15	- .06	+1.21	+ .242
18. Kota	+0.57	+3.35	+1.24	+1.72	+1.78	+8.66	+1.732
19. Nagaur	- .16	- .38	- .43	- .59	- .54	-2.10	- .42
20. Pali	+ .88	- .25	+ .10	+ .14	+ .06	+ .93	+ .186
21. S. Madhopur	- .52	- .09	- .36	- .39	- .38	-1.74	- .348
22. Sikar	- .71	- .57	- .55	- .62	- .58	-3.03	- .606
23. Sirohi	- .69	- .62	- .53	- .63	- .59	-3.06	- .612
24. Sri Ganganagar	+1.45	- .05	+ .48	+ .52	+ .34	+2.74	+ .548
25. Tonk	- .62	- .61	- .51	- .06	- .56	-2.36	- .472
26. Udaipur	+ .73	+2.71	+ .11	+ .96	+ .91	+5.42	+1.084
Σx	2132	1473.2	191817	10407.5	13649		
$\overline{X}$	82	56.66	7377.58	400.29	524.96		
SD	104.8	84.63	12882.307	619.08	875.48		

APPENDIX TABLE 4E.3: Water Supply Power Consumption Trends

Districts	1979-80		1984-85		1989-90	
	mkWh	% of total	mkWh	% of total	mkWh	% of total
1. Ajmer	17.727	13.3	26.230	12.0	34.733	11.45
2. Alwar	2.090	1.5	4.549	2.1	7.008	2.31
3. Banswara	1.243	0.9	1.615	0.7	1.987	0.65
4. Barmer	2.650	2.3	9.530	4.4	16.410	5.41
5. Bharatpur	1.389	1.1	2.167	1.0	2.945	0.97
6. Bhilwara	2.061	1.6	3.773	1.7	5.485	1.81
7. Bikaner	10.877	8.1	15.509	7.1	20.141	6.64
8. Bundi	1.740	1.3	2.645	1.2	3.550	1.17
9. Chittor	2.424	1.8	4.173	1.9	5.922	1.95
10. Churu	5.984	4.5	9.783	4.5	13.762	4.54
11. Dungarpur	1.211	0.8	1.711	0.8	2.211	0.73
12. Jaipur	29.010	21.8	44.001	20.2	58.992	19.45
13. Jaisalmer	0.904	0.7	2.829	1.3	4.754	1.57
14. Jalore	1.699	1.3	2.486	1.2	3.273	1.08
15. Jhalawar	1.465	1.1	1.806	0.8	2.147	0.70
16. Jhunjhunu	4.307	3.2	5.350	2.5	6.393	2.12
17. Jodhpur	14.241	10.6	25.148	11.5	36.055	11.89
18. Kota	8.141	6.1	14.804	6.8	21.467	7.08
19. Nagor	4.594	3.4	7.360	3.4	10.126	3.34
20. Pali	2.754	2.1	5.361	2.4	7.968	2.63
21. S. Madhopur	2.054	1.5	2.804	1.3	3.554	1.17
22. Sikar	3.510	2.6	4.828	2.2	6.146	2.03
23. Sirohi	1.562	1.1	1.568	0.7	1.574	0.52
24. Sri Ganganagar	2.391	1.8	7.655	3.5	12.919	4.26
25. Tonk	1.395	1.1	2.373	1.1	3.351	1.10
26. Udaipur	5.925	4.4	8.168	3.7	10.411	3.43
Total	133.348	100.0	218.316	100.00	303.284	100.00

APPENDIX TABLE 6B.1: Areal Differentiation Pattern of Energy System in Rajasthan, Districtwise Distribution as on 31 March 1986

Districts	Consumer ('000) X1	Con-sumption (mkWh) X2	Trans-former ('000kVA) X3	Villages Electri-fied X4	Harijan Basti electrified X5	Wells ener-gised X6
1. Ajmer	129.0	261.6	449.0	639	420	11094
2. Alwar	89.4	364.8	637.1	1356	251	18834
3. Banswara	29.8	37.6	145.6	679	177	3079
4. Barmer	24.6	52.7	95.6	337	118	2656
5. Bharatpur	57.3	75.4	338.3	778	311	7806
6. Bhilwara	77.7	153.5	465.5	1224	934	13049
7. Bikaner	75.2	78.3	153.1	390	223	31
8. Bundi	33.0	58.2	231.8	539	146	4190
9. Chitor	82.4	197.7	509.3	1258	599	23810
10. Churu	55.4	42.9	313.7	451	282	511
11. Dholpur	12.5	22.2	56.7	245	177	1131
12. Dungarpur	26.9	14.1	48.9	479	76	2073
13. Jaipur	334.6	770.6	1669.7	1956	720	53777
14. Jaisalmer	5.7	12.3	16.4	47	34	21
15. Jalore	40.7	94.9	217.7	495	384	10799
16. Jhalawar	38.4	44.2	310.2	680	528	7744
17. Jhunjhunu	74.2	269.2	211.1	650	401	15487
18. Jodhpur	114.6	235.6	605.2	554	223	6790
19. Kota	113.5	505.8	1011.1	1177	367	6952
20. Nagor	83.0	162.7	441.7	884	343	12011
21. Pali	94.9	150.4	297.6	763	545	13946
22. S. Madhopur	58.9	111.5	235.2	891	432	12057
23. Sikar	102.6	250.6	592.3	810	474	22602
24. Sirohi	39.8	126.2	193.9	420	269	6194
25. Sri Ganganagar	120.1	199.8	385.1	1066	459	4923
26. Tonk	34.1	30.0	100.5	448	344	4623
27. Udaipur	129.1	485.2	595.7	1665	785	15795
Total	2077.4	4808.0	10328.8	20881	10022	281985
$\overline{X} = X/n$	76.94	178.07	382.55	773.37	371.18	10444
SD	61.903	175.87	336.87	432.22	212.11	10718.0

APPENDIX TABLE 6B.2: Areal Differentiation Pattern of Energy System in Rajasthan; District wise percentage of Total; as on 31 March, 1986

Districts	Consumer X1	Consumption X2	Transformer X3	Villages electrified X4	Harijan Basti electrified X5	Wells energised X6
1. Ajmer	6.22	5.44	4.35	3.06	4.19	3.93
2. Alwar	4.28	7.59	6.17	6.49	2.50	6.68
3. Banswara	1.43	0.78	1.41	3.25	1.77	1.09
4. Barmer	1.18	1.10	0.93	1.61	1.18	0.94
5. Bharatpur	2.76	1.56	3.28	3.73	3.10	2.77
6. Bhilwara	3.74	3.19	4.51	5.86	9.32	4.63
7. Bikaner	3.62	1.63	1.48	1.87	2.23	0.01
8. Bundi	1.59	1.21	2.24	2.58	1.46	1.49
9. Chittor	3.97	4.11	4.93	6.02	5.98	8.44
10. Churu	2.67	0.89	3.04	2.16	2.81	0.18
11. Dholpur	0.60	0.46	0.55	1.17	1.77	0.40
12. Dungarpur	1.29	0.29	0.46	2.29	0.76	0.74
13. Jaipur	16.10	16.03	16.17	9.37	7.18	19.07
14. Jaisalmer	0.27	0.26	0.16	0.23	0.34	0.01
15. Jalore	1.96	1.97	2.11	2.37	3.83	3.83
16. Jhalawar	1.85	0.92	3.00	3.26	5.27	2.75
17. Jhunjhunu	3.57	5.60	2.05	3.11	4.00	5.49
18. Jodhpur	5.52	4.90	5.86	2.65	2.22	2.41
19. Kota	5.46	10.52	9.79	5.64	3.66	2.46
20. Nagor	3.99	3.38	4.28	4.23	3.42	4.26
21. Pali	4.58	3.13	2.88	3.65	5.44	4.95
22. S. Madhopur	2.83	2.33	2.28	4.27	4.31	4.27
23. Sikar	4.94	5.22	5.73	3.88	4.73	8.01
24. Sirohi	1.93	2.62	1.88	2.01	2.69	2.20
25. Sri Ganganagar	5.78	4.16	3.73	5.11	4.58	1.75
26. Tonk	1.65	0.62	0.97	2.16	3.43	1.64
27. Udaipur	6.22	10.09	5.76	7.97	7.83	5.60
Total	2071.7	4808.0	10328.8	20881	10022	281985

APPENDIX TABLE 6E.3: Income and Expenditure on Power: After Appropriation (Figures in Crores of Rs.)

Year	Revenue Receipts	Revenue Expenditure	Net Loss (-) Surplus (+)
1957-58	1.32	1.57	(-) .25
1958-59	1.41	1.81	(-) .40
1959-60	1.58	1.90	(-) .32
1960-61	1.88	2.05	(-) .17
1961-62	2.44	2.61	(-) .17
1962-63	3.08	3.89	(-) .81
1963-64	5.07	5.19	(-) .12
1964-65	5.86	6.63	(-) .77
1965-66	6.59	7.67	(-) 1.08
1966-67	7.28	9.65	(-) 2.37
1967-68	10.12	13.41	(-) 3.29
1968-69	13.93	16.14	(-) 2.21
1969-70	16.26	17.12	(-) .86
1970-71	20.34	20.65	(-) .31
1971-72	24.10	26.17	(-) 2.07
1972-73	25.96	31.16	(-) 5.20
1973-74	32.88	40.11	(-) 7.23
1974-75	43.37	47.90	(-) 4.53
1975-76	51.77	53.41	(-) 1.64
1976-77	75.66	66.37	(+) 9.29
1977-78	98.79	98.68	(+) .11
1978-79	103.09	108.02	(-) 4.93
1979-80	130.93	143.78	(-) 12.85
1980-81	132.38	149.28	(-) 16.90
1981-82	120.55	173.11	(-) 52.56
1982-83	156.52	207.61	(-) 51.09
1983-84	213.82	284.75	(-) 70.93
1984-85	225.54	321.66	(-) 96.12
1985-86	319.64	365.21	(-) 45.57
1986-87	403.82	413.31	(-) 9.49

APPENDIX TABLE 7A.1: Levels of Electrification in Rajasthan (1986) Standardised Values

Distt.	X1	X2	X3	X4	X5	X6	ΣX	ΣX/n
1. Ajmer	+ .84	+0.47	+0.20	-0.31	+0.23	+0.06	+1.49	+ .25
2. Alwar	+ .20	+1.06	+0.75	+1.34	-0.56	+0.78	+3.57	+ .59
3. Banswara	- .76	-0.79	-0.70	-0.22	-0.91	-0.68	-4.06	- .68
4. Barmer	- .84	-0.71	-0.85	-1.01	-1.19	-0.73	-5.33	- .89
5. Bharatpur	- .32	-0.58	-0.13	-0.01	-0.28	-0.25	-1.57	- .26
6. Bhilwara	+ .01	-0.14	+0.24	+1.04	+2.65	+0.24	+4.04	+ .67
7. Bikaner	- .03	-0.56	-0.68	-0.88	-0.69	-0.97	-3.81	- .64
8. Bundi	- .71	-0.68	-0.45	-0.54	-1.06	-0.58	-4.02	- .67
9. Chittor	+ .09	+0.11	+0.37	+1.12	+1.07	+1.25	+4.01	+ .67
10. Churu	- .35	-0.77	-0.20	-0.74	-0.42	-0.93	-3.41	- .57
11. Dholpur	-1.04	-0.88	-0.96	-1.22	-0.91	-0.87	-5.88	- .98
12. Dungarpur	-0.81	-0.93	-0.99	-0.68	-1.39	-0.78	-5.58	- .93
13. Jaipur	+4.16	+3.37	+3.82	+2.74	+1.64	+4.04	+19.77	+3.29
14. Jaisalmer	-0.58	-0.47	-0.49	-0.64	-0.06	+0.03	-2.21	- .37
15. Jalore	-1.15	-0.94	-1.08	-1.68	-1.59	-0.97	-7.41	-1.24
16. Jhalawar	-0.62	-0.76	-0.21	-0.22	+0.74	-0.25	-1.32	- .22
17. Jhunjhunu	-0.04	+0.52	-0.50	-0.28	+0.14	+0.47	+0.31	+ .05
18. Jodhpur	+0.61	+0.33	+0.66	-0.51	-0.69	-0.34	+0.06	+ .01
19. Kota	+0.59	+1.86	+1.86	+0.93	-0.02	-0.33	+4.89	+ .82
20. Nagor	+0.98	-0.08	+0.17	+0.26	-0.13	+0.15	+1.35	+ .22
21. Pali	+0.29	-0.16	-0.25	-0.02	+0.82	-0.33	+1.01	+ .17
22. S. Madhopur	-0.29	-0.38	-0.44	+0.27	+0.29	+0.15	-0.40	- .07
23. Sikar	+0.41	+0.41	+0.62	+0.08	+0.48	+1.13	+3.13	+ .52
24. Sirohi	-0.60	-0.09	-0.56	-0.46	-0.48	-0.40	-2.59	- .43
25. Sri Ganganagar	+0.69	+0.12	+0.01	+0.68	+0.41	-0.52	+1.39	+ .23
26. Tonk	-0.69	-0.84	-0.84	-0.75	-0.13	-0.54	-3.79	- .63
27. Udaipur	+0.84	+1.74	+0.63	+2.06	+1.95	+0.50	+7.72	+1.29
Σ	2077.4	4808.0	10329	20881	10022	281985		
$\overline{X}$	76.94	178.07	382.55	773.37	371.18	10444		
SD	61.903	175.87	336.87	432.22	212.11	10718.8		

$$SV = \frac{X - \overline{X}}{SD}$$

APPENDIX TABLE 7B.1: State Domestic Product versus State Power Consumption

Year	NSDP crores Rs.	Per capita income Rs.	NSPC mkWh	Per capita use kWh	Per capita kWh: Rs.
1972	1464.3	570	1104.5	42	1:13.57
1973	1568.4	594	1261.6	47	1:12,64
1974	2058.7	759	1331.4	48	1:15.81
1975	2132.8	765	1564.4	55	1:13.91
1976	2192.9	767	1822.6	63	1:12.17
1977	2700.7	907	2107.4	71	1:12.77
1978	2956.7	969	2267.9	74	1:13.10
1979	3194.8	1023	2724.8	87	1:11.75
1980	2912.0	1013	2968.9	93	1:10.89
1981	4121.0	1220	2928.9	90	1:13.55
1982	4977.7	1429	3131.4	90	1:15.88
1983	5853.7	1634	3168.8	91	1:17.95
1984	7397.5	2011	4148.7	115	1:17.48
1985	7517.6	1990	4386.5	119	1:16.72
1986	7920.6	2043	4808.0	124	1:16.47

Source: Budget Studies and Power Reports (1972-1986).

Measurement of Coefficient using the formula:

$$r=\frac{\Sigma XY-\frac{\Sigma X\Sigma Y}{N}}{\sqrt{\Sigma X^2-\frac{(X)^2}{N}}\ \sqrt{\Sigma Y^2-\frac{(Y)^2}{N}}}$$

Correlation Coefficient between NSDP and NSPC

$$=\frac{192.06-\frac{58.9\times 39.9}{15}}{\sqrt{301.69\ \frac{(58.9\times 58.9)}{15}}\ \sqrt{125.33-\frac{(39.9\times 39.9)}{15}}}$$

$$=\frac{35.39}{36.76}=0.962,\quad R^2=926,\quad t=12.88$$

Correlation Coefficient between per capita income and power:

$$=\frac{159.72-\frac{175.94\times 12.09}{15}}{\sqrt{2444.75\ \frac{(175.94\times 175.94)}{15}}\ \sqrt{10.7189-\frac{(12.09\times 12.09)}{15}}}$$

$$=\frac{17.91}{19.268}=0.9295,\quad R^2=0.864,\quad t=9.087$$

BIBLIOGRAPHY

Action, J.P.; Mitchell, B.M. and Mowill, R.S., (1976). *Residential Demand for Electricity in Los Angeles: An Economic Study for Disaggregated Data*. Rand Corporation (R-1899-NSF) Santa Monica, Calif. (September).

Alekseev, G.N., (1986). *Energy and Entropy*, Mir Publication, Moscow.

Anderson, K.P., (1972). *Residential Demand for Electricity: Econometric Estimates for California and the US*. The Rand Corporation (R-905 NSF), Santa Monica, Calf. (January).

Alagh, Y.K.; Bhaduri, A. and Bhalla, G.S., (1978). *Agricultural Growth and Manpower Absorption in India. Labour Absorption in Indian Agriculture – Some Exploratory Investigation*, International Labour Office Bangkok.

Blattenberger, G.R., (1977). *The Residential Demand for Electricity*. Department of Economies, University of Michigan, Ann Arbor (December).

Chapman, D.; Mount, T. and Tyrell, T., (1972). *Electricity Growth: Implications for Research and Development and Electricity Demand in the United States*. Oak Ridge National Laboratory, Oak Ridge, Tenn. (June).

Cater, A.P., (1974). Energy, Environment and Economic Growth. *The Bell Journal of Economics and Management Science*, 5, No. 2 (Autumn); 578-592.

Denny, M.G.S. and Pinto, C., (1975). *The Demand for Energy in Canadian Manufacturing: 1949-70*. University of Toronto.

Douglas Evans, (1978). *Western Energy Policy*, The Macmillan Press Ltd., London.

Foley, G. and Nassim, C., (1976). *The Energy Question*, Penguin Books.

Gapay, Les, (1974). Weighing All the Energy Options, *Wall Street Journal*, December 13, pp.12.

Henderson, P.D., (1975). *India: The Energy Sector*, Oxford University Press.

Hammond, R. and McCullagh, P.S., (1977). *Quantitative Techniques in Geography*, Oxford.

John Silk, (1979). *Statistical Concepts in Geography*, George Allen & Unwin, London.

Jorgenson, D.W.; Berndt, E.R. and others, (1973). U.S. Energy Resources and Economic Growth. Report to Energy Policy Project, Washington, D.C. (September).

Kundu, A. and Raza, M., (1982). *Indian Economy: The Regional Dimension*, Spektrum Pub., N. Delhi.

Llyinykh, I.I., (1985). *Hydroelectric Stations*, Mir Publishers, Moscow.

Magidin, F., (1986). *Construction of Power Transmission Lines and Substations*, Mir Publishers.

Mahmood, A., (1977). *Statistical Methods in Geographical Studies*, Research Publications, N. Delhi.

Mehta, B.C., (1983). *Structure of Rajasthan's Economy*, Research Books, Jaipur.

Moulik, T.K., (1982). *Biogas Energy in India*, Academic Book Centre, Ahmedabad.

NCAER, (1966). *Demand for Energy in India*, NCAER, N. Delhi.

O'Toole, (1978). *Energy and Social Change*, The MIT Press, Cambridge.

Parikh, K.S., (1977). Projecting and Planning India's Fuel Requirement. International Studies of the Demand for Energy Ed. W.D. Nordhaus, North-Holland Publishing Co., New York, Oxford, pp.213-236.

Rajput, M.S., (1985). *Agriculture Productivity in India*. Discovery Publishing House, Delhi.

Robert Mabro, (1980). World Energy Issues and Policies. Proceedings of the First Oxford Energy Seminar (Sept., 79), Oxford University Press.

Sing, A., (1983). *Desert Resources and Technology*, Vol. I, Scientific Publishers Jodhpur.

Tyner E. Wallace, (1978). *Energy Resources and Economic Development in India*. Martinus Nijhoff Social Sciences Division, Leiden/Boston.

Venikov, V.A. and E.V. Putyatin, (1978). *Introduction to Energy Technology*, Mir Publishers, Moscow.

Willy Brandt, (1980). *North-South: A Programme for Survival*, Pan Books London and Sydney.

INDEX